More Advance Praise for *BiblioTech*

"In *BiblioTech*, John Palfrey sums up the seminal function libraries have played in inspiring and preserving creative thought over the ages. Then, with confident optimism, Palfrey makes it counterintuitively clear that the digital age has expanded the function and energy level of libraries. In a splintered world, these book-centric institutions have also become singularly safe and welcoming tech havens where the public can seek knowledge and gain access to wide-ranging perspectives about events and circumstances, real and fictional. It is the library where the imagination is un-shackled, where the past and present can be civilly probed and the future contemplated, alone or together in community. As a society we shortchange these civilizing institutions at our peril."

> —*Jim Leach, former Chair of the National Endowment*
> *for the Humanities*

"Whether you think you know a lot about libraries today and in the future—or feel clueless about both issues—you will be enlightened by John Palfrey's thoughtful, timely, and lucid presentation."

> —*Howard Gardner, Hobbs Professor of Cognition and*
> *Education at the Harvard Graduate School of Education*

"John Palfrey insightfully charts the information revolution's path through the world of libraries, where he has been an innovator. We are indeed at an exciting moment."

> —*Tony Marx, President and CEO of the New York Public Library*

"*BiblioTech* is a call to arms to foster democracy by supporting libraries. John Palfrey takes the reader on a library journey from the libraries of antiquity through the Carnegie era and into the digital age and beyond. He challenges all of us to keep the library relevant—as an information re-source, cultural archive, a community gathering place, and most power-fully, as a cornerstone of democracy for an informed citizenry."

> —*Amy Ryan, President of the Boston Public Library*

"In *BiblioTech*, John Palfrey challenges the library and archival commu-nities to pursue new strategies to shape, rather than be shaped by, the digital revolution. This is a call to action for these institutions to reinvent themselves to meet the challenges of tomorrow's world. *BiblioTech* argues for the creation of a new nostalgia, one that reaffirms the essential role of these institutions in a democratic society—to inform, to engage, and to delight."

> —*David S. Ferriero, Archivist of the United States, former*
> *Andrew W. Mellon Director of the New York Public Libraries*

"In *BiblioTech*, John Palfrey offers fresh perspectives and keen insights on the importance of libraries in the digital age. He reaffirms the value of libraries as purveyors of knowledge and information in democracies around the world. Yet, he reminds us that we must leverage our core values and skills as collaborators, networkers, and community builders for libraries to remain relevant. *BiblioTech* is a call to action for libraries to claim their role as key innovators in learning, addressing digital literacy, and bridging the technology divide in order to thrive in the Age of Google."

　　—*Luis Herrera, City Librarian of the San Francisco Public Library*

"John Palfrey has crafted a bold new vision and compelling argument for the power and value of public libraries. Perhaps more importantly he warns us of the unfortunate future for free societies if we simply stay the course and don't 'create a new nostalgia' for the digital age. Many speeches have been given and books written on the topic of the 'future library,' but this is the finest and most inspiring call to true action I've read. *BiblioTech* should be required reading for not only every librarian, but every library supporter and policymaker."

　　—*Deborah L. Jacobs, former City Librarian of the Seattle Public Library*

"*BiblioTech* is a must read for anyone who cares about the future of libraries. John Palfrey has eloquently identified the essential role libraries play in keeping our democracy strong and has clearly articulated the challenges facing libraries today. This is a true wake-up call. We may very well fail our communities and society if we do not invest in library innovation that supports access and preservation of knowledge at scale."

　　—*Susan Hildreth, former Director of the Institute of Museum and Library Services*

"One of America's top educators and library leaders makes a passionate argument for why libraries in the digital age are more important than ever to our democracy. In a lucid, conversational style that draws on his unique knowledge and experience, digital library pioneer John Palfrey offers a penetrating analysis of how libraries must transition to a digital, collaborative, and networked future while preserving the best of their traditional physical advantages. An urgent, eloquent call for the public option—indeed, the public obligation!—to step up and manage this historic shift to the digital future so that every member of society has equal access to knowledge and information that is responsibly presented and preserved for the benefit of all."

　　—*Doron Weber, Vice President of Programs and Program Director at the Alfred P. Sloan Foundation*

Biblio
TECH

Why Libraries Matter More
Than Ever in the Age of Google

JOHN PALFREY

BASIC BOOKS
A Member of the Perseus Books Group
New York

Published by Basic Books
A Member of the Perseus Books Group

Set in 11.5 point Minion Pro

Library of Congress Cataloging-in-Publication Data

Palfrey, John G. (John Gorham), 1972–
    BiblioTech : why libraries matter more than ever in the age of Google / John Palfrey.
        pages   cm
    Includes bibliographical references and index.
    ISBN 978-0-465-04299-9 (hardback)—ISBN 978-0-465-04060-5 (e-book) 1. Libraries and the Internet. 2. Libraries—Social aspects—United States. 3. Library information networks. 4. Libraries and electronic publishing. 5. Library users—Effect of technological innovations on. 6. Librarians—Effect of technological innovations on. 7. Digital preservation. 8. Libraries—Forecasting. I. Title.
    Z674.75.I58P38 2015
    020.285'4678—dc23   2014041874

10 9 8 7 6 5 4 3 2

For Catherine

Contents

Introduction

IN 1852, JOSHUA Bates wanted to help the city of Boston start the first major public library in the world. Bates, a businessman and civic-minded citizen, had a few conditions in mind. The library, he wrote, ought "to be an ornament to the city." It should have a capacious reading room, one that could accommodate 100 to 150 readers at a time. And most important, the library was to be "perfectly free to all." If the trustees of this new institution agreed with the conditions set forth in his letter, Bates was happy to provide $50,000 to buy the books.

With the help of Bates and other donors, the Boston Public Library (BPL) became the first library to allow any citizen of a major city in the United States to borrow books and materials. This idea seems obvious today; in 1852 it was radical. Libraries had existed for thousands of years, of course. Early libraries, such as the Library of Alexandria in present-day Egypt, served very small communities of readers, ordinarily people associated with a monastery or a court. The Bodleian Library at Oxford University opened to scholars in 1602. Private libraries—including the Library Company of Philadelphia, founded by Benjamin Franklin in 1731, and the Boston Athenaeum, founded in 1807 just down the street from the new BPL—allowed the well-to-do to share books with one another. But it was not until the middle of the nineteenth century that a big city opened a library to *all* its citizens. To commemorate the spirit of this new library, and with a nod to Mr. Bates and his gift, three words were inscribed above the main door to the Boston Public Library's iconic main building: FREE TO ALL.[1]

The free municipal public library in America has spread far and wide from its roots in Boston's Copley Square. Free public libraries cropped up quickly across the young country, from the town of Woburn in the Boston suburbs to small towns in New York State. The plan for the massive New York Public Library, in the heart of Manhattan, came together in 1895. The philanthropist Andrew Carnegie took this idea across the country when he offered to pay for the construction of public libraries in any town that would meet a few conditions. By 1917, Carnegie had promised to build 1,679 libraries in 1,412 towns across America. Carnegie sought to establish town libraries that were free, ubiquitous, and accessible to those who shared his own character traits: industry, ambition, and eagerness to learn.[2]

Today every major city in the United States and most cities around the world have a public library system devoted to making knowledge broadly accessible. Most other free countries also have extensive public library systems. As in America, public libraries spread across Britain during the middle of the nineteenth century, especially after Parliament passed the Public Libraries Act 1850. (A handful of public libraries had already been established in Europe—including Chetham's Library in Manchester, England; the Saulieu Library in France; and the Zaluski Library in Warsaw, Poland—several claiming to be the first town to offer a public library.) Travel just about anywhere today and you will see that books, magazines, and DVDs—along with much more—are freely available to anyone with a library card. The town center of nearly every community has a library, with story hours for children, tax forms and voter registration materials for new citizens, and caring librarians who welcome everyone to a safe space on a hot day. In the United States, thousands of these libraries look the same, inspired by the original Carnegie library designs, a comforting fixture of American small-town life.

But in the digital era, the classic public library is long overdue for an update. The original design of libraries—as glorified storehouses for books and manuscripts and pleasant places to read them—no longer suffices. People have many more options today to get access to knowledge. The job of librarians is changing under their feet in this new world.

The Boston Public Library is no different. For starters, the library's space needs to change. In 1972 the BPL added a new building, designed by famed architect Philip Johnson. At the time the Johnson building was hailed as a triumph of modern design. Today, however, it feels hulking and impersonal, the product of a distant era—one in which library design apparently did not focus much on the experience of human beings. The Johnson building did little to convey the grand and open spirit of the original McKim building, the historic front door to the Boston Public Library. The McKim building evokes awe and wonder as the visitor enters its grand entryway. Inside, the visitor is greeted by John Singer Sargent's mural sequence: painted over a thirty-year period, *Triumph of Religion* reaches toward the heavens. To the visitor entering the library from Boylston Street instead of from Copley Square, the entrance to the Johnson building sends quite a different signal—utilitarian, at the most generous.

In 2012 the library's director, Amy Ryan, and her colleagues Michael Colford, Gina Perille, and Beth Prindle decided to do something about the Johnson building. They set about the business of remaking it by asking Boston residents what they thought needed to change. The response from the public was revealing—and damning. Some people said the Johnson building was so confusing that they "couldn't find a book to read." Others reported that the space was not welcoming to young people—the demographic in Boston, as in many communities, most likely to need and use the library. The layout was confusing and disjointed. Spaces devoted to the materials that patrons most wanted to use, and perhaps borrow, were set back too far inside the large building, behind a maze of walls. The message sent by the architecture was not one that Ryan wanted patrons to receive—it did not signal a welcoming and vibrant space. The BPL leaders knew they couldn't afford to ignore such clear feedback.

Ryan and her team of librarians and architects—this time from William Rawn Associates—came up with an exciting design for a new public library that has galvanized public support. This new design makes the impersonal Johnson building much more inviting and connected to the surrounding community. Floor-to-ceiling windows will transform the space from one with a warehouse feeling to one that draws people into the building from the sidewalk. The BPL's redesign calls for a teen-friendly digital media lab that will allow young people to read books, do their homework, hang out, and make things. It will also have a space for tween readers who may feel too young to use the teen space. An early childhood center will be stocked with developmentally appropriate toys as well as books, music, and other materials. Fiction, movies, and music will be brought closer to the entryway—historically a cold, empty space—for adult patrons to browse. A coffee cart will attract those in need of a dose of caffeine.

The city threw its weight behind the redesign. Boston's longtime mayor Thomas Menino pledged that money would be there for the renovation. Sure enough, the city council approved $16 million for the first phase of work. Under equally strong leadership from the next mayor, Marty Walsh, the next $60 million followed in 2014. The city of Boston has rallied around its library and is doubling down as the BPL overhauls itself for a new era.

In addition to the redesign of its main building, the Boston Public Library has been busily remaking its other services. New branches in neighborhoods around the city—another innovation that the BPL brought to the world of libraries—have been added to the system. Through a project called the Digital Commonwealth, the BPL is home to a digitization project that is bringing images, books, maps, and manuscripts to the web from every corner of the state and preserving them for posterity. Photos of small-town high school girls' basketball teams are now as easily available online as photos of a glamorous professional tennis star who grew up in Boston. These images are now a click away for those looking into the history of gender equity or for the relatives of the high school athletes. A series of local historical maps of Gloucester and of the state of Massachusetts show changes in the fishing industry over time and their effects on the lives of coastal residents. It would have been impossible for any one city or town to bring these digital materials to life; a collaborative effort, led by the BPL and its partners, has created a new library model for the nation, one that combines the physical with the virtual.

The Boston Public Library is a great example of a major modern library embracing its future. Even the BPL's inspiring efforts are only the beginning of what will be possible when libraries seize the opportunities of the networked digital age. Nevertheless, the BPL's leaders and all others seeking to reinvent libraries for the future are also working against some powerful headwinds.

L IBRARIES ARE AT risk because we have forgotten how essential they are. In the era of Google and Amazon, those with means can access information with greater ease and speed than ever before. As a consequence, in cities and towns across the world the same debate rages each year when budget time rolls around: What's the purpose of a library in a digital age? Put more harshly, why should we spend tax dollars, in tough economic times, on a library when our readers can instantly get so much of what they need and want from the Internet? As the bulk of funding for police, fire departments, and schools—all necessary services—has become the responsibility of state and local governments, municipal leaders have been forced to ask a question that library supporters aren't prepared to answer: are libraries necessary?

We keep having this debate because we have a very simplistic and skewed idea of why libraries matter. For most of us, libraries are good for one thing: getting information. But most information today can be readily accessed in digital form, through computers or smartphones. How many times recently have you had a debate with a friend, only to resolve the dispute within seconds simply by pulling out a mobile device and looking up the answer? Most of the information that we need in our day-to-day lives can now be found in both analog (meaning "physical") form and digital form. Most of the time, the digital variants can be accessed by anyone, easily and quickly, from anywhere, using a mobile device. Acquiring the physical variants often requires more effort—an actual trip to the library, for instance.

The point is not that books, magazines, and DVDs are dead—far from it. At places such as the redesigned Boston Public Library, popular publications and media materials in physical form circulate rapidly from prominent spaces close to the building's entrance. The point is that people's information habits have undergone a sea change—a major shift toward the digital. Libraries are trying to serve a wide range of patrons at many different points along an "adoption curve," with all-print at one end and all-digital at the other. A related shift is also under way: libraries must increasingly compete with commercial establishments that offer free wireless Internet access and a place to gather, such as Starbucks. In the midst of all this change, libraries of all sizes and types are forced to make the case for their own relevance. The problem is that libraries need to provide both physical materials and spaces as well as state-of-the-art digital access and services.

Our views about what libraries offer are firmly entrenched, which makes the task before library supporters even harder. If most knowledge is accessible in digital formats, on devices that can be carried anywhere, what is the purpose of a traditional library collection of books, journals, magazines, movies, and music? If the Internet is the primary access point for this information, what is the purpose of preserving physical spaces where people can come to find it? If libraries are nothing more than community centers in cities and towns and on college campuses, then what do we need librarians for? Put in negative terms: Are libraries and librarians anachronistic in a digital age? Who, after all, are they serving, and how?

Libraries are more than community centers, just as librarians do more than answer questions you could easily ask Google. From the opening of the BPL, the first public library, to the expansion of public libraries across America through the Carnegie libraries, the library as an institution has been fundamental to the success of our democracy. Libraries provide access to the skills and knowledge necessary to fulfill our roles as active citizens. Libraries also function as essential equalizing institutions in our society. For as long as a library exists in most communities, staffed with trained librarians, it remains true that individuals' access to our shared culture is not dictated by however much money they have.

For many citizens, libraries are the one place where the information they need to be engaged in civic life is truly available for free, requiring nothing more than the time to walk into a branch. The reading room of a public library is the place where a daily newspaper, a weekly newsmagazine, and a documentary film are all available for free. In many communities, the library's public lecture room is the only place to hear candidates for office comparing points of view or visiting professors explaining their work on climate change, immigration, or job creation. That same room is often the only place where a child from a family without a lot of money can go to see a dramatic reading or a production of a Shakespeare play. (Another of these simple realities in most communities is that a big part of public librarians' job is to figure out how to host the community's homeless in a safe and fair manner.) Democracies can work only if *all* citizens have equal access to information and culture that can help them make good choices, whether at the voting booth or in other aspects of public life.

Libraries, then, are core democratic institutions today just as they were in the nineteenth century. The knowledge that libraries offer and the help that librarians provide are the lifeblood of an informed and engaged republic. This role for libraries is just as important in big cities like Boston and New York as it is in every small town in every democracy. From the rise of the public library system in late-nineteenth-century America, libraries have been the place where any citizen could go to pursue his or her own interests, free of cost.

The disappearance of libraries as we know them would affect the way our children are educated—for the worse. It would undercut the ability of immigrants to any free country to adjust well to a new system, find jobs, and join the ranks of literate working-class and middle-class citizens. Libraries provide public spaces where people can congregate, share their common cultural and scientific heritage, and create knowledge. Librarians, along with archivists, maintain the historical record of our societies and our lives. By failing to invest in libraries during this time of transition away from the analog and toward the digital, we are putting all these essential functions at risk just when we need them most.

T HE PATH FORWARD for libraries and librarians is not
mysterious. Visionary leaders like Amy Ryan and her
team at the Boston Public Library are charting the way forward. A reinvestment effort by Siobhan Reardon at the Free
Library of Philadelphia has resulted in a $25 million grant to
reimagine her city's library. Many other librarians—in school
libraries, universities, and special libraries, at technology
companies and nonprofits—are likewise showing the way.
The key is very simple: to focus on what digital media and the
Internet make possible, not on what they undo. This perspective enables library supporters to find and exploit the ways in
which the digital and the analog come together, where they
reinforce one another. The Internet and digital media are enabling new kinds of services that make a real difference for
all library users: for instance, librarians can find, at no cost,
interactive materials ranging from original historical documents to the notes from recent city hall meetings. Physical libraries have never been more vital, interesting, useful
places. The people who work in libraries are helping other
people make sense of the overwhelming mass of information
online—and making it immediately relevant to their lives.

We need both physical libraries and digital libraries today. Physical spaces and digital platforms will both play an
essential role in providing access to knowledge in democracies around the world in the near future. If we don't maintain physical libraries, we will lose essential public, intellectual
spaces in our communities, places where people can meet
face-to-face, and if we don't build digital libraries connected

to them, those physical spaces may become obsolete as big companies such as Google and Amazon increasingly meet our need for knowledge. Physical and digital libraries are interdependent: each can make the other more effective and valuable.

T HERE ARE FEW, if any, more diverse communities in the world than the borough of Queens in the city of New York. That diversity is on clear display at its public libraries. At the Forest Hills branch library, you may not be able to find a seat on a Saturday afternoon. Patrons of many races and ages sit elbow to elbow among computer terminals. There are books there, too, on tables and in low bookshelves that line the wall, but the eye doesn't go to the books in the room. What you can't help but notice is that most of the patrons are sitting at computers. The place is not quiet either; chatter fills the crowded room. It's a productive and vibrant sound, not unhappy. The predominant activity most definitely is not looking for and reading books.

The changing atmosphere in libraries, which is not limited to Queens and other big-city environments, does not spell doom for libraries. Public libraries in cities and towns across America, as well as school and university libraries, are changing their spaces and their rules to accommodate shifts in the ways people access and relate to information. Today library spaces are often vibrant—for some, too vibrant—and many libraries are setting records for attendance, circulation of materials, and provision of access to ideas and events.

The need for access to knowledge has never been greater than it is today. Although no one disputes that access to knowledge is a good thing in modern democratic societies, the problem is that access to this knowledge is unevenly distributed. Libraries, and librarians, can be a central part of solving that distribution problem if we support them and push for innovation, instead of more of the same.

THE BOSTON PUBLIC Library and the Queens Borough Library are not outliers, but neither are they the norm. Across America and the world, libraries are in peril. Not every big-city mayor is pledging to "find the money" for a top-to-bottom renovation of historic library buildings. Queens, despite the public demand for its library system, has been among the places hardest hit over the past decade by cuts to its libraries, a leadership scandal, and controversies over spending. Too many mayors and town managers, forced to make hard budget choices, are slashing library budgets to save other essential services.[3]

Libraries of all kinds are facing budget pressures. Worried about spiraling tuition increases, college presidents are freezing pay in libraries, reducing the rate of new book purchases, and laying off librarians and archivists. Public school libraries are under the greatest budget pressure of all in some parts of the country: they have responded by firing librarians, reducing the number of books they buy, limiting the hours that they are open, and closing school libraries outright. Library buildings are being repurposed as community centers and even bed-and-breakfasts. The important cultural heritage institutions that are keepers of unique records in communities and often partner with libraries—such as archives and local historical societies—are also struggling to keep their doors open. We now run a very high risk of failing to maintain complete historical records, especially those held in digital formats.

While the job of remaking physical libraries is best accomplished one at a time, with a view toward the needs of the particular community, developing digital library platforms ought to be a highly collaborative process. Individual librarians need not work alone to find fresh ways to use new technologies to reinvigorate their library's services. Large-scale digital initiatives make possible extraordinary new forms of library services. For years librarians have bandied about the possibility of creating a "digital Library of Alexandria." Today that project is finally under way. With massive digital libraries becoming sources of knowledge, inspiration, and innovation for the global community, the possibilities are breathtaking.

It is unlikely that a single global digital library will emerge. Dozens of governments and groups of librarians are developing national-scale digital library platforms, especially in Europe, East Asia, and the United States. A series of nationally or regionally interconnected digital library platforms will not replace physical libraries but rather will support librarians and open up new opportunities for libraries to focus on the work they do best, without requiring each of them to develop redundant infrastructure and unique collections. Developing digital library platforms is a massive project, and they are taking some time to come to fruition, but one thing is clear: libraries are already innovating in important ways. Our job now as citizens and library patrons is to support them in their efforts so they can fulfill their essential role in our communities. Libraries are well on their way to becoming networked organizations that can thrive in the years to come.

THIS BOOK PROJECT began while I was the director of a library. I was what people in the library business call a "feral"—a nonlibrarian who ends up working in a library. I was a law professor and a director of a research institute, the Berkman Center for Internet and Society at Harvard University. I focused my teaching and writing on the ways in which our use of digital technologies can transform democratic institutions. I have long been fascinated by the changes wrought across our society by our growing use of information technology. My boss at the time, then-dean of Harvard Law School and now a US Supreme Court Justice, Elena Kagan, offered me the job of running the world's largest academic law library, and I jumped at the chance.

I began my career as a library director by admitting how little I knew about how libraries operate and how much I needed to learn. Over the past decade or so, I've read widely in the academic literature about library and information science. More important, I've met with many hundreds of people who work in and around libraries and with others who care a lot about libraries too. This book has also been enriched by a series of interviews conducted with some of the most innovative librarians in this country and around the world. I emerged from my experience as a library director with deep respect for librarians—as well as for the "ferals" who work in libraries.

Since 2010, I have also been working, along with many others, to establish a national digital library system for the United States. The Digital Public Library of America, or DPLA, brings together the cultural and scientific heritage of the United States in digital form. It is large-scale, highly distributed, and incredibly ambitious. Collaboratively designing the DPLA took over two years of open meetings and involved thousands of people throughout the country, both in person and online. This book is informed by the years of conversations during the DPLA planning process that ensued when we asked: how do we develop a shared system that enables all of us to benefit from the scale and access that digital technologies make possible but that also retains the local touch and personal connection that have long been the specialty of physical libraries? (As fate would have it, the DPLA's physical offices are nestled within the BPL's Johnson building—the same building undergoing a total overhaul.)

Now, at the end of this learning process, I find myself at once excited and worried about the future of the profession and about libraries as institutions. There is so much that libraries and librarians can offer in a digital age; much of it is already a reality, and on the horizon is even more that we cannot envision today. Unfortunately, we tell survey researchers how much we value and love libraries, but we do too little to support them. Libraries are much like the environment in this respect: we say we care deeply about clean air, clean water, and reversing the harm associated with climate change, but we somehow continue to vote for people who do little to carry out our good intentions.

Support for libraries, both financial and otherwise, is crucial during this period of transition from a predominantly analog to a predominantly digital world. All of us, especially nonlibrarians, need to consider the important role of libraries in our lives and in the shared lives of our communities. At the same time, libraries themselves, as institutions, need to take advantage of changes in the digital environment. Though many libraries are making these changes, too many others are not; moreover, some of these changes are not ambitious enough, or they're poorly coordinated. Some librarians will no doubt chafe at my recommendations, upset that they are not getting enough credit for the change already under way in their institution, whether it's a library, archive, historical society, or other cultural institution. It may be true that they are not getting enough credit, either here in this book or elsewhere, but my target audience is everyone else—all those who do not work in libraries and who should be taking a greater interest in the fate of these essential knowledge institutions on which we rely more than we seem to realize.

Above all else, this book is a celebration of libraries. I make the case for what libraries can do for people of all ages and from all walks of life, even—and especially—in a digital age. There is much to love about the libraries of the past. With ample reason, most people harbor warm feelings about the libraries they have frequented. But as libraries undergo the necessary changes described here, we should honor, support, cheer, and fund those library leaders who are well ahead of the curve as they continue their excellent work. Other librarians who are deeply unsure of themselves as they adjust to radically different circumstances need our support as well.

Though a celebration of libraries, this book also administers a dose of tough love. With a sensibility primarily focused on possibilities rather than nostalgia, I look ahead to the libraries of the future and propose what may be some uncomfortable changes for current institutions if they are to thrive. But this is by no means a hopeless project. In any conceivable version of the digital future that emerges, both libraries and librarians are absolutely necessary. Libraries must, and can, reinvent themselves as institutions.

As citizens, we need to support our libraries during this transition time by encouraging library reform geared toward meeting the needs of our communities and communities across the world. We also need to be ready to foot the bill for library reform—as private citizens, as institutional leaders, and as taxpayers. Just as it took individuals like Benjamin Franklin and Joshua Bates to pay for the founding of the great libraries in America, we will need a new generation of library philanthropists to step up for the digital age. Philanthropy certainly has a role to play at this time of transition, but ultimately, in every free republic, the state needs to support libraries as an essential public good. In America, that means that the Congress, the state legislatures, and municipal governments should all be stepping up to fund libraries more than they are today. Compared to most other shared public costs, such as education, security, and health care, libraries do not require big money. In relative terms, tiny public investments in libraries go a very long way.

Individual libraries are remaking themselves into collaborative and much better connected organizations, but more librarians need to get involved and collaborate with each other to an extent that was unnecessary in the past. Such collaboration will establish networked digital library systems that can help to meet many of the historic aims of libraries without undercutting the system of writing, publishing, and library support that has served societies well in the analog past. Until then, these vast, expensive, ambitious projects to bring about large-scale digital library systems around the world need to come together. In the United States, the Digital Public Library of America today is up and running, growing quickly, and becoming one of the building blocks in a new world for libraries in a digital age. Similar projects are in the planning or operating stages in countries around the world. There is no reason why these national programs cannot be connected into an international network—a worldwide library platform in the service of the global public.

Libraries are in danger because they are caught between two ideas that are not easily reconciled: on the one hand, the public sentiment that the digital era has made libraries less relevant, and on the other, the growing number of expectations we have for libraries, stemming in no small part from the very digitalization that the public assumes is making them obsolete. These two ideas cannot both be right.

Much turns on how well we manage this transition from an analog to a digital world, and the fate of libraries hangs in the balance. If we do not have libraries, if we lose the notion of free access to most information, the world of the haves and the have-nots will grow further and further apart. Our economy will suffer, and our democracy will be put at unnecessary risk. Everyone has a stake in the future of the libraries, archives, and historical societies that safeguard our culture and inspire our people.

Chapter One

Crisis

A Perfect Storm

Libraries are screwed. Libraries are screwed because we are invested in the codex [the traditional book format]. And the codex has become outmoded.

—Eli Neiburger, "A *Library Journal/School Library Journal* Online Summit," September 29, 2010

A S A NEWLY appointed library director, I was amazed at the number of times I had the exact same conversation with friends at backyard barbecues and cocktail parties. It went something like this.

FRIEND: Oh, how interesting, you're now the director of a library? I thought you were a law professor. You're not even a librarian.

ME: Yes, I am very excited about the challenge, and no, I am not trained as a librarian.

FRIEND: But wait. We don't really need libraries so much now that we have Google, right?

ME: No, actually I think we need them more than ever—

FRIEND (*cutting me off*): Oh, now I'm getting it. You're the digital guy, and you're coming in to get rid of the library, right? Now this all makes sense.

I'd start again with my reply about the growing, not diminishing, importance of libraries, but I'd get nowhere.

People in the United States still have very positive views of libraries, but those views rest too heavily upon a sense of nostalgia. We remember libraries as they were twenty, thirty, fifty years ago, as quiet, inviting places to read and learn. There's no question that libraries are wonderful, but nostalgia is too thin a reed for librarians to cling to in a time of such transition. Nostalgia can actually be dangerous. For one thing, thinking of libraries as they were ages ago and wanting them to remain the same is the last thing we should want for them. For another, our nostalgic view doesn't give libraries enough credit. Libraries offer a whole slew of services that we ignore when we just focus on pleasant reading rooms.

The profound threats to libraries today are not merely a result of our own misperceptions but stem from meaningful shifts in society. It sounds like a cliché, but it is worth stating plainly: we live in a time of rapid and transformative changes in the world of publishing, information technologies, and learning. The changes in each of these areas have been brought about by the transition from an analog-based world of atoms to an increasingly digital and highly networked world in which bits play a greater and greater role in virtually every aspect of modern life.

The changes wrought by the digital revolution add up to a perfect storm for libraries and librarians. Every kind of librarian—whether in a public library, a school library, a major research university, or an archive—faces a series of problems that can't all be solved at once using the resources they have today. This perfect storm is so terrifying because the role that many librarians have seen for themselves historically is not a great fit for the current era. In ages past, librarians saw their job as "collectors" and "keepers" of information. These tasks were easier in the past than they are today because of the relative scarcity in the past of information that was available to be collected, kept, and made accessible.[1]

For the libraries of antiquity, the amount of recorded information that they could collect was extremely small by comparison to today's world of information overload. Think of the library at the palace of Ebla, in what is now modern-day Syria. This early library, one of the first on record, operated between about 2600 and 2300 BC. Its collection, among the largest of its era, consisted of about 17,000 tablets. The library's holdings, essentially archival materials, covered administrative, legal, and commercial topics. The library also held hymnals, dictionaries, and epic narratives. The scale of what could be collected, even by a monarch, was modest. This collection of tablets fit in two rooms of the palace.[2]

In early libraries, part of the job of librarians was to gain access to other libraries so that they could copy information by hand (or, if necessary, steal it). A primary means of adding to the Library of Alexandria's collection—much larger than Ebla's—was by fiat. Any ship that landed in the port of Alexandria had its books confiscated so that they could be copied and then returned. Alexandria's library wasn't the only one built this way. Stephen Greenblatt's best-selling history *The Swerve* tells the story of a fifteenth-century Italian scholar named Poggio Bracciolini who traveled throughout Europe seeking monasteries that might have hidden treasures that he could somehow spirit back to his native country. The essence of Poggio's job was to collect recorded knowledge and bring those original copies to another location. The point was to make this information available to be consulted, in person, by scholars and nobles.[3]

The printing press changed just about everything in publishing, but not all that much in the way libraries operated. Modern libraries continued the tradition of their earlier counterparts in preserving the historical, cultural, and scientific record and making it available to some of the most privileged members of society. Even in the centuries that followed the introduction of the modern printing press, the number of titles printed was still relatively small, and the reading public was limited to the very wealthy or the unusually well educated. Librarians could serve a very useful function by accumulating and cataloging an amount of information that one scholar could get his (almost always a male back then) mind around. These functions were extremely important, but the benefits they offered were far from evenly distributed throughout society.

The mass democratization movement in the nineteenth century changed the field of libraries forever. In Boston the new public library replaced the pay-for-access, Brahmin-dominated Athenaeum as the primary source of recorded information and the keeper of the city's cultural and historical record. The example of the Boston Public Library was quickly emulated in many other towns and cities, especially elsewhere in the northeastern part of the United States. Henry Hobson Richardson, among the most famous architects of his time, traveled extensively through Europe and brought back designs to New England. A series of iconic libraries designed by Richardson, based on the Episcopal vicarages and other buildings he had loved in Europe, would spring up on the village greens of towns in Massachusetts, such as Woburn and Quincy.

By the early part of the twentieth century, the traditional notion of the library as a "treasure chest" or "jewel box" to preserve knowledge for the select few had given way to a far more democratic mission. The library became a central point in a community—whether a small town or a big city, a small college or a grand research university—where anyone could pursue knowledge and skills, with the help of trained professionals. The jewel box model was largely replaced by the lively, open, exciting institution we can visit today, one that is tied directly to the community—and in turn, to the success of the democratic system.

Now libraries are changing yet again, and the job of a librarian today has become vastly harder than it was in the past. Libraries and the publishing world are inextricably linked, and the rate of change in virtually every aspect of librarianship and publishing is now unusually high. Today we measure developments in the information and publishing business in terms of months, years, and decades rather than centuries, as we did in the past. Hundreds of years passed between the invention of movable type in China and Gutenberg's press in Germany; it was another few centuries before many people could afford to own printed Bibles or the other offerings of the modern publishing industry. In contrast, Moore's Law—the claim that computer processing speed doubles every eighteen months—has held up remarkably well as a theory over the past five decades. The invention of the personal computer ushered in today's world of near-ubiquitous digital information, but the information and technology landscapes have not stood still: they are constantly being fundamentally altered—by all of us, by how we use information and how we use technologies.

The amount of information published around the world in both printed and digital formats continues to rise each year, in both academic fields and with respect to literature meant for public consumption. More than 1 million books are published each year around the world—more than any library would consider acquiring on its own. The fastest-growing segment of the book world is self-publishing, which has tripled in the past five years in the number of titles published, rising to more than 200,000 by 2012. At the same time, the amount of information published on the web has grown at an even faster rate.[4]

Libraries are in crisis not only because it is impossible to collect and catalog the vast quantities of printed and digital material that are being published every year, but also because it is prohibitively expensive even to attempt it. Libraries are expected to provide more services, across more formats, than ever before, but with fewer resources. Library staff and budgets are being squeezed at every level, from the best-endowed university library to the smallest local public library, school library, or town historical society. No one can pay the bill for all the material that libraries are expected to provide access to for their patrons. Moreover, the cost to libraries of providing that access to this expanding amount of information is also growing extraordinarily fast. The primary reason for this cost increase is the multiplicity of formats: with information now available in a growing number of formats, libraries are forced to decide which formats are worth acquiring.[5]

Libraries also now struggle with the problem of who, exactly, should count as a publisher. Big publishing houses—Penguin Random House, say, or Perseus, the publisher of this book—are no less important than they once were as arbiters of what should be printed and read. A library in Los Angeles, for instance, must provide access to the *Los Angeles Times* as well as *La Opinion,* the largest Spanish-language newspaper in the United States, and perhaps other major newspapers of record, such as the *New York Times, Der Spiegel,* and *Le Monde.*

But from there, it gets much more complicated. "Publishers" now include individuals making their work available through blogs, personal websites, and social networks. Universities have become publishers through their institutional repositories in addition to their traditional presses. Governments and companies publish official information on the Internet in what may be exactly the form that library users are looking for—not a traditional printed book.[6]

In today's world the sources of information that matter most to library users will sometimes be these nontraditional publishers. Consider the terrible earthquakes that struck Japan in 2011, or the devastation caused by Hurricane Sandy to the New York area in 2012. In both cases, traditional publishers and newspapers have issued much information worth gathering for readers. But so, too, have individuals who posted video from their smartphones, still photographs on Flickr or Instagram, and firsthand accounts on blogs, Tumblr, Twitter, and Facebook. The historical and cultural value of these individual accounts—"user-generated content"—is obvious. Libraries can't afford to buy all the material that is formally published while also curating everything that is informally published. Whether they pick one or the other, someone is always disappointed. Librarians today are in an impossible spot.

The problem for librarians stems from the hybrid nature of today's information. The library of 2014 is not entirely digital. Nor, in all likelihood, will most libraries be entirely digital for the foreseeable future. The near-future of libraries will be a hybrid of yesterday's predominantly print-based world and tomorrow's primarily digital world.

For the time being, then, we occupy a "digital-plus" information environment. The central idea is that new works are, and will continue to be, created and stored in digital formats as a default. As I wrote and edited this book, for instance, I created it as a digital file. Later, the original digital information was rendered into multiple formats, including a printed book, which you might hold in your hands, and an ebook, a different digital format that might appear in your Kindle. The dominant mode of information creation and access continues its shift from analog to digital with each passing year. We create and access almost all information, at least as a starting point, through digital means.

The nature of the demand for library materials is changing, mostly toward the digital. Our modes of teaching, learning, and research are changing along with the format changes. In the context of formal education, both experiential and hands-on modes of education continue to change rapidly. Many law schools, for example, have revamped the traditional curricula that have been in place for a century by adding more clinical teaching and problem-solving approaches to understanding the law. The same is true for business schools, which are adopting more experience-based, global approaches to learning. With these new, hands-on forms of learning come new and flexible formats for teaching materials, such as digital case studies, interactive websites, and video collections.[7]

Librarians play a central role in supporting these new modes of teaching, learning, and scholarship. Academic libraries are expected to support "digital scholarship," using sets of "big data." Empirical research continues to grow across a wide range of fields, from business and economics to law and history. Librarians, too, are taking on the job of curating materials in a fast-expanding range of digital formats. Patterns of information use by students, faculty, and practitioners are in a state of flux, giving rise to new claims on the time of librarians.[8]

Consider a university that wants to attract and support scholars interested in the digital humanities, a rapidly growing area of inquiry. The digital humanities, as a field, enables scholars to bring a new set of tools to the work of understanding the human condition. It is as though a new microscope were all of a sudden available to biologists. Through the digital humanities, scholars are able to analyze massive bodies of text in new ways and to bring the originals of the rarest texts in the world into any classroom, anywhere. With these new tools, research and teaching in the humanities are both changing rapidly at the hands of ambitious scholars. However, the new digital services can be extremely expensive to provide to scholars. The costs of supporting digital scholarship, for instance, include new budget lines for three items: staff (or at least staff retraining in the form of professional development), technological infrastructure, and access to proprietary data.

To make matters both more complex and harder still for librarians, there are multiple types of "digital humanities," each with its vocal proponents. There is the "big digital humanities," which takes its cues from the fast-growing areas of science and the corporate obsession with "big data." (The title of an October 2012 *Harvard Business Review* article put this newfound focus in clear terms: "Data Scientist: The Sexiest Job of the 21st Century.") The combination of access to large sets of data in digital format—such as text—and computing tools that can find patterns within them opens new doors for scholars. Others argue that the beauty of the digital humanities lies in smaller-scale, higher-touch, extremely creative uses of archival materials that can be analyzed and presented in revealing new ways.

For either type of work in the digital humanities, big or bespoke, librarians are called upon to offer new services to their scholarly patrons. To take a simple problem, imagine a scholar of history and literature who wants to use a new computer system to compare the works of Marlowe to the works of Shakespeare. The big data scenario requires skills on the part of librarians in finding and providing access to data sources (the literary texts that can be subjected to computerized analysis) that rarely can just be ordered from a publisher. In a much harder problem, imagine that the scholar wants to compare all the poetry recorded in the Elizabethan era. To meet this demand, libraries would often have to pay hefty fees for data, pulling the funds for this new purchase out of accounts otherwise reserved for buying books. Even assuming that librarians are able to obtain these data, additional problems crop up. Libraries rarely have the technical infrastructure to catalog these data, present them to scholars, and preserve them over the long term. And even if they do, the publishers of such data are often unwilling to sell the rights to the data for the long term.

Most challenging of all, not all humanists at a university wish to practice the craft of digital humanities; they expect all the wonderful library services they have received in the past to support their classical mode of scholarship. Should the library director support the tenured faculty member who wants the university to continue to collect all European monographs in printed form? Or the newly hired assistant professor who is seeking expensive data sets, new computers and software, and support in understanding the latest techniques in natural language processing?

Ideally, libraries would not have to choose between the needs of the tenured professor and the assistant professor and could have all the good things they have today and also build for tomorrow. But the facts make this approach untenable. The challenges in funding and support that libraries face every year, in every context, suggest that such wishful thinking is unwise.

During this transition, librarians can't immediately get rid of print in order to focus only on digital. Print and other analog formats are not disappearing. Some users continue to print out materials to read them, to carry them around, and to mark them up by hand. Others use printed copies of books as a starting point to begin their research, as they have in the past. Others want to access rare and unique materials found in special collections—to touch the paper, to smell the must, to examine the handwriting in the margins. The paper-based format can facilitate access to information in ways that remain critical.[9]

When they listen carefully to library users, librarians come to the conclusion that they need to collect and provide access to *both* print and digital materials. But they do not have the money or the staff to do either job as well as any-one would like. Many books and serial publications are still only available in printed format. Many materials will always remain in printed form, such as manuscripts in archives, printed texts held in special collections, and books held as objects of study. The original copies of unique and rare ma-terials will continue to require labor-intensive (and loving) physical care. We may also digitize these works, however, to enable broader access and to help preserve them.

Meanwhile, major library systems will need to continue their role as stewards of distinct materials rather than as col-lectors. As stewards, a library system looks after a set of ma-terial in physical form on behalf of society at large. That role is different than collecting copies of all material. Although it would be nice for every university or major city library to have a copy of all material that anyone might possibly want to consult, that model is already too hard to keep up—and is getting harder to maintain with every passing year. A network of stewards can accomplish vastly more than a disconnected (even sometimes competitive) group of collectors ever can.

This distinction between stewards and collectors will be-come more important, not less so, over time. New knowledge today, in contrast to what has come before, is largely born digital. Librarians are new to the task of preserving and providing access to these digital materials, but they have had to learn quickly. The newest data sets created today—unorganized or minimally structured raw data—are principally digital in format. Young library users in particular are shifting their focus beyond text to encompass audio and video files, as well as interactive files, more than libraries do today. Researchers are also increasingly using primary sources such as blogs, visual images, sound recordings, and websites. It would be a terrible mistake to assume that everyone creating this digital information is planning to preserve it. Think, for instance, of the blogger who described the corruption she observed in a Kenyan election, or a videographer who happened to capture the first big waves breaching the levees of New Orleans during Hurricane Katrina. Start-up publishing companies are focused on easy ebook distribution and almost certainly don't have a hundred-year-plan for digital preservation. These digital materials will need to come under the purview of library collections, both to provide immediate access and for long-term preservation.[10]

The shift to primary materials that are predominantly born digital brings with it a series of long-term problems for librarians that have yet to be solved. New formats, for instance, are often less stable than their earlier counterparts. One of the scariest propositions in a digital age is the concept of "data rot." The Library of Congress, which holds roughly 150,000 compact discs of audio recordings, estimated that between 1 and 10 percent of the CDs already had serious data errors as of 2003. People still worry about long-term access to the US census of 1960, which was recorded on what are now obsolete computer tapes.[11]

Another reason why print cannot go away immediately is because it continues to play a key role in the preservation of knowledge. There is reason to fear that we will lose much of the digital information that we are creating—and perhaps exactly the material we most want to preserve—at a terrifying rate. We are much better at creating digital information than we are at storing it. Court records, for instance, are often created as digital files but then stored as physical books because librarians fear losing the digital versions more quickly than the analog. Librarians and archivists often emphasize the need to take precautions with digital materials. One approach is to print out backup copies of born-digital materials and store them in a safe place for the long term to mitigate the risk of data rot.[12]

Consider the challenge to libraries, archives, and historical societies of collecting the emails of prominent figures in society. We run the acute risk today of preserving far less, not more, of today's historical record because of the way the information is created, stored, and typically discarded before it is copied or given to libraries for safekeeping. Many libraries are hard at work figuring out how to preserve the emails of key figures for posterity, despite the multiplicity of email clients (programs such as Microsoft's Outlook or Mozilla's Thunderbird that help us manage our email), the changes in email formats that are bound to come, and the many formats in which attachments and embedded or linked files may appear. This challenge—of keeping up with new data formats and fast-changing information usage patterns—is likely to increase, not decrease, over time if the recent past is any guide.[13]

As a library director at Harvard, I worried a lot about the effectiveness of our digital archiving methods. For instance, both of my bosses at Harvard Law School, Elena Kagan and Martha Minow, handled much of their correspondence via email, as do most other professionals today. I fear that we will have much better records for the deanship of Christopher Columbus Langdell, who led Harvard Law School at the end of the nineteenth century, than we will for Dean Kagan or Dean Minow in the early twenty-first century. The same might be said of the correspondence of Harvard President Drew Faust. A historian, President Faust wrote a pathbreaking book about death that draws upon the letters sent home from the front during the American Civil War, entitled *This Republic of Suffering*. Unless we come up with new strategies, Faust's own electronic correspondence, recorded 150 years later in history, may be less accessible in the future than the bloodstained letters recovered from the 1860s. We may be left to wonder if there are lost emails of David Foster Wallace that will never resurface the way lost letters of J. D. Salinger did in 2013, three years after his death in 2010.

THE ESSENTIAL CHALLENGE for libraries is to balance a broad and growing slate of activities that span the analog and the digital. Without infinitely growing budgets, it is impossible to continue to acquire more materials each year, in more formats, at rising costs. These changes are taking place at the same time that the global economy has proven especially volatile, particularly since the tailspin induced by the credit crunch in the second half of 2008. Public funds are in short supply. There is no end in sight to the shrinking of budgets, staff, and space in libraries. No library is immune from these pressures: even in the few cases where library budgets remain stable, the prices for the same materials continue to rise from one year to the next.[14]

Budget cuts today are the norm for many libraries. The University of California–San Diego library system reported that it lost nearly 20 percent of its state funding over a recent five-year period, sustaining $5 million in cuts. A survey by *Library Journal* showed that 72 percent of libraries had experienced budget cuts in fiscal year 2010, with 43 percent of those surveyed cutting staff as a result. The highly effective and respected Queens Borough Library in New York City— home to the vibrant branch library in Forest Hills—had to close fourteen branches, cut three hundred staff jobs, and reduce hours in 2010 as a result of budget cuts.[15] The budgets of school libraries, which make up the bulk of the libraries in the United States, have been among the hardest-hit in recent years. The American Library Association (ALA) maintains a depressing web page that chronicles the budget cutting at public libraries across the country.[16] In the 2012 *Library Journal* budget survey, libraries reported that they continued to tread water in budgetary terms, with modest cuts to materials budgets and modest increases to cover cost-of-living increases for existing staff.[17] The best that librarians can reasonably expect today is to maintain or slightly increase the levels of funding after an era of brutal cuts.[18]

IT IS NOT possible for even the most creative librarian to do all the work of the analog past—providing all the services that library users have come to expect and to associate with great libraries—while also inventing the new digital future. Such an undertaking would be impossible even if budgets were climbing rapidly. There is a solution, however, one that requires libraries to accept the task at hand and join forces with libraries across the country to carry it out successfully. Libraries have no choice but to collaborate in acquiring and preserving materials, far more ambitiously than they have in the past, in order to meet the challenges presented by rising costs. Libraries also need to cooperate on the development of the technologies and the services that will make them relevant for the near-term future.

This period of transition for libraries will be hard and expensive. It will require a great deal of innovative thinking, unpleasant trade-offs, and changes in lots of jobs for lots of people. But it will pay great dividends to society, if done right, just as investments in libraries have proved wise—and paid off handsomely—for centuries.

Chapter Two

Customers

How We Use Libraries

A library card is the start of a lifelong adventure.
—Lilian Jackson Braun

A ninth-grader—age fourteen—came into my office with a proposal to make. Today I am the principal of a high school, blessed with extremely bright students from around the world. After figuring out who the Apple Computer school sales representative was for our region of the United States, this student had been engaged in an extended conversation with the rep about our school buying iPads for all students. Neither I nor any other administrator at the school was involved at all in these conversations, which came as something of a surprise.

When the student came into my office to propose that the school buy iPads for all our students, he came with a list of the pros and cons associated with changing from print-based textbooks, used by most teachers, and the digital alternatives beginning to emerge on the market. He had thought it all through. This student recited chapter and verse about the benefits to kids of iPad-based curricular materials rather than traditional printed texts: interactivity, better tailoring to student ability levels, better fit with contemporary student learning styles, and less strain on students' backs and arms from the backpacks nearly all of them wore on campus.

This student could not understand why I wouldn't just demand that all faculty immediately begin teaching all courses from iPads. Why wouldn't we just switch over all at once and rely on electronic textbooks?

After hearing him out, I explained why we wouldn't be switching immediately to a digital format for teaching materials. But even though I didn't agree with his plan in its entirety, I did learn some things from him: he liked to engage with information, and he had sound reasons for caring so much about using iPads to learn. After all, it is the demand side of the education equation—not just the supply side, from teachers and administrators like me—that really matters in the end. Teachers know best, in very many respects, and our authority and knowledge are plainly important. But we don't know everything. Student interest and passion can be the lifeblood of any great school.

Libraries need to take the time to ask hard questions about how their patrons are seeking knowledge and using information differently than they have in the past.

Our institutions of learning—including libraries and schools, even journalism—risk falling out of step with the generation of people coming of age today. Libraries need to adapt to the changing information habits of their users. The problem is that these changes are happening very quickly for some and less quickly for others. Libraries serve a diverse range of patrons with a diverse set of practices, ranging from the most digitally savvy to the determinedly analog. We may think we know what all patrons want from libraries, but preferences are changing every year. Dynamism must be the watchword for libraries in a digital age.

L IBRARIES ARE NOT alone among the institutions needing to make a massive transition to the digital age. This same challenge hit the telecommunications industry, the movie industry, and the newspaper industry, among many others, starting in the late 1990s. The publishing industry, journalism, and education are facing similar issues today. Some have responded well and are thriving; others have suffered and continue to struggle. Libraries need to take cues from the ways others have responded—and especially those that have made missteps along the way.

Consider what happened to the recording industry. In 1999 a student at Northeastern University, Shawn Fanning, unleashed a disruptive force called Napster, the first major peer-to-peer-style sharing network for audio files. In a matter of months, Napster's meteoric rise had tipped the scales against an old distribution model for recorded entertainment in favor of a new, direct, and digital model. The music industry (in)famously took years to embrace this change, initially fighting Fanning and all those who saw the world the way he did. The recording industry sued both the disrupters—which were plainly seeking to profit from illegal acts—and tens of thousands of their customers who were unlawfully uploading and downloading copyrighted songs. This set of legal battles raged for the better part of a decade, and in the end they were a colossal waste of time. The net result was a lot of money spent on lawyers and lobbyists, a lot of money being made by one computer company, Apple, and the emergence of an almost exclusively digital mode of production, distribution, and consumption of recorded music.

The analogy between recorded music and printed books in a digital age is imprecise. What has happened with music has not yet happened with books, although a shift is on in reading patterns too. A clear trend in the growth of ebook circulation over a four-year period can be seen in the figures supplied by the service provider OverDrive: 4 million ebook checkouts in 2010 grew to 16 million in 2011, 54 million in 2012, and 79 million in 2013. Set in percentage terms, the numbers are even more staggering: the increase between 2010 and 2013 was 1,875%. Despite this clear and rapid growth, the number of physical books lent from libraries still towers over ebook lending overall (63 percent to 4 percent of all lending, according to one recent study). Another sign of complexity in the book marketplace is that many book lovers continue to have a passion for shopping at independent bookshops, even if they sometimes read books on their Kindles.[1]

Usage patterns in libraries vary according to media type. Music and newspapers are primarily consumed in their digital formats: few people check out print newspapers or CDs—especially not new and popular music—from libraries. Movies (as DVDs) still circulate in large numbers, however, even as movies-on-demand, delivered digitally to consumers, are on the rise.[2] This split in media usage patterns is excellent news for libraries. It buys time for change to take place within libraries as institutions; it buys time for librarians to gain new skills and come up with new strategies; and it means that libraries can continue to meet immediate needs using traditional analog approaches.[3]

If the trends in readership and learning patterns continue, this reprieve for libraries will be temporary. The expectations of library users, of all ages, are changing with the times. Librarians, of course, have noticed. The services that librarians offer today are often creative and inspiring, a far cry from what most people expect from libraries. But at too many libraries changes in services are happening at the margins, not at the core. The shift in the information practices of library users is far outpacing the digital shift in libraries. If libraries are to get ahead of these changes, we as taxpayers and library patrons need to support them in this transition. And we have ample reason to do so: for starters, our children and grandchildren use libraries more than any other age group.

WHEN A CHILD first walks into a library, she is struck with a sense of wonder. If she is lucky, she finds herself in a well-lit, lovely space, surrounded by books, music, and film. She soon comes to see the world as bigger, more complex, and more intriguing than she has yet experienced. Her world expands, in real time, as she listens to someone read to her, as she learns to read herself, and as she chooses what she wants to read on her own. In the lives of many children, libraries play an essential role in the unfolding of the world around them.

As she recalls her childhood years later, memories of how her imagination exploded as she walked through the open door of a library may rank among her most powerful mental images. She will associate that original sense of wonder with the hushed, open spaces; the smell of the books and the stacks (and perhaps the must of old libraries); the kind suggestion of a parent or librarian; the long afternoons getting pulled into the pages of an engaging story while tucked away in a corner of a cozy public space. Perhaps she will remember the library as a cool safe haven away from the crowds and bustle of a hot, noisy, possibly dangerous city. Years later, as part of the retelling, she might even exaggerate a bit when describing the central role that the library played in her young life. She wouldn't be the first to do so, and she'd be forgiven her rhetorical flourishes.

The celebrated British author Zadie Smith has said that she owes her "whole life to books and libraries," given their importance during her childhood. In telling an interviewer for *The Guardian* that libraries are "absolutely essential," she argued in terms of equity and access to opportunity. "A lot of people don't have books on their shelves," Smith noted. "The library was the one place I went to find out what there was to know."[4]

One library supporter (and now a law professor), Esme Caramello, told me that she will always associate libraries with orange soda. Growing up in the Midwest, she came from a family that was devoted to reading and opposed to junk food. Her local library, in Highland Park, Illinois, ran a contest for students who read a certain number of books over the summer. The prize was a party in August at which the library would serve orange soda out of a huge plastic container, much like the sort that football players tip over the heads of their coaches after winning a championship game. All summer long, young Esme could taste the orange soda as she cruised through book after book.

Today children are still fortunate enough to have such eye-opening (and mouth-watering) experiences, even if the library looks different than it did when today's adults were growing up, and even if children today use libraries in vastly different ways. It seems counterintuitive, but in this age of Google and Facebook, surveys show, young people are going to libraries even more often than those who are older.[5] This is excellent news, and it portends good things for society at large. The experience of exposure to a broader world of knowledge, in the physical space of a library, remains very much a part of growing up in a free society.

In wired societies, the experience of children today is hybrid, caught somewhere between the analog experiences of their parents and the almost certainly digital experiences their own children will have someday. For young people who are learning in both a digital environment and the physical world, there is a strong sense of convergence between the two. For these children, physical life and online exploration are not separate worlds. Their reality is not "online life" and "offline life"—it's all just "life."

The news coming out of the research community about libraries is almost unequivocally positive. Despite the cries of poverty by public funders of libraries and the corresponding financial pressure that libraries face as institutions, public support for libraries—especially as institutions geared toward children—remains high. These findings are validated, year after year, in survey after survey. In a survey conducted in 2013, more than 90 percent of Americans felt that libraries play a vital role in communities. In particular, Americans think that libraries should focus on serving kids. Few public institutions receive favorability ratings as high as libraries do.[6]

The best news for librarians out of this research is that they are succeeding in bringing young people through their front doors. Young people are by far the most likely group, by age, to use libraries today. In a 2011 Pew survey, 72 percent of high school students ages sixteen or seventeen reported that they had used a library in the past year. Sixteen- and seventeen-year-olds are the age group most likely to read daily for work or school, at 95 percent. That number is higher than it is for any other age bracket, including the elderly and others one might guess would use libraries more frequently than kids. For instance, in the same study, fewer than half (49 percent) of those over age sixty-five reported that they had used a library in the previous twelve months. Young people still use libraries, and they use them in large numbers—driven largely, it turns out, by school assignments. Studies show that students benefit from working with librarians while doing their research. Students who are proficient at searching for information online often report that they were explicitly taught research skills by a librarian or teacher.[7]

If the data about library usage are so positive—especially among digitally savvy youth—then one might reasonably ask: why is a "tough love" approach necessary and urgent? The problem is that these data about library popularity, including among young users, tell only part of the story. Getting young people through the front door is a starting point, but it will not be enough over the longer term. Just as they still want printed books, library users want change too. They are embracing technological approaches to getting and creating knowledge. Library users tell survey researchers that they want access to more ebooks and they want libraries to offer more technologically up-to-date services.

The problem today is that there is a looming disconnect between what some libraries continue to offer and what students are telling researchers they want. Data concerning the research practices of today's students, conducted by Project Information Literacy in 2009, offer a starting point for forward-thinking librarians. Consider the learning style today of a typical American college student. In one important national survey from 2010, students age eighteen and older said that they turn to friends and family to begin their research and to help them evaluate the quality of information they find. When the research is for a specific class, not surprisingly, they first turn to their course readings. They are also very likely to turn to Google, Wikipedia, and other online services that provide access to information they need for their research projects. Additionally, if consulting a person, students prefer to ask a teacher for advice about research information before consulting a librarian. However, when students team up with librarians as part of their school research, they are more likely in the future to use research databases than Google.[8]

As the surveys conducted by Project Information Literacy make plain, students think to ask for help from a librarian long after they have sought support from others, including Google and Wikipedia. Libraries are far from the first place that many students look for information when beginning to research a new topic. As the survey's investigators wrote:

> Almost all of the respondents turned to the same set of tried and true information resources in the initial stages of research, regardless of their information goals. Almost all students used course readings and Google first for course-related research and Google and Wikipedia for everyday life research. Most students used library resources,

especially scholarly databases for course-related research and far fewer, in comparison, used library services that required interacting with librarians.[9]

Even outside of school, kids are learning in informal, digitally mediated ways that supplement their in-school experiences. In other words, the digital experience is presenting kids with learning opportunities that are entirely outside of the formal structure of school-based education systems. Often these experiences are provided by schools themselves or nonprofits, but the institutions seeking to take advantage of the learning that kids are willing, and even eager, to do online also include smart companies, such as Rupert Murdoch's NewsCorp. NewsCorp's education strategy calls for kids to learn grade-school material almost exclusively through a tablet, much like an iPad, with both carefully curated information and access to the Internet at large.[10]

As kids get older, they continue to find informal modes of learning that help them develop deep and rich interests. According to a 2013 study co-released by the Pew Internet and American Life Project and the Berkman Center for Internet and Society, 25 percent of all American teens go online, mostly using a phone. Among teens who own a smartphone, 50 percent are using the Internet primarily through their phone. Students are learning as they ride city buses, fiddling with their mobile devices, and as they multitask late at night, watching television while on Facebook and texting their friends. They are learning in many of the massively multiplayer online role-playing games (MMORPGs)—games that bring large numbers of players together into a virtual online world to compete simultaneously—that they frequent, often for hours per day. This learning is not all good—some of it involves taking on very bad habits, which we need to counteract—but much of it is extremely productive. Educators, including librarians, are just starting to explore serious ways of tapping into this vein of informal learning.[11]

IN ADDITION TO following the lead of students and their specific interests, librarians can play a crucial role in reducing the "digital divide" between those who have access to fast Internet and those who do not, which still persists. Over the past decade, libraries have played an essential role in providing free, fast Internet access to those who cannot otherwise afford it. This role may be a temporary one—Internet coverage may someday be as universal as electricity—but we are not there yet, neither here in the United States nor in almost all other countries.

Although young people have more ways than ever to access the Internet, access to high-speed broadband connections remains unevenly distributed, according to a wide range of studies. Since the advent of the World Wide Web in the early 1990s, policymakers and academics have worried a lot about the digital divide—the notion that the well-off are more likely to have access to advanced technologies and the network itself than those who are less-well-off. Although Internet service is much more available today than at any other

time in the past, especially through network-connected mobile devices and a growing series of options for getting network access at home, divides persist. According to a 2013
Pew study, 90 percent of college graduates in the United
States had high-speed Internet access, compared to less than
34 percent of those who had not finished high school. Related
concerns are the type, speed, and nature of access to information. Well-off consumers in most densely populated areas can choose from various options to get fast broadband in
their home through their cable or satellite provider, and even
through their electric utilities in some places, but not every-
body is so fortunate.[12]

High-speed connection to the Internet is very expensive
all around the world. On a global level, only about one-third
of the world's population has access to the Internet. In the
United States, study after study has confirmed the obvious
fact that many people simply cannot afford high-speed Internet connections even if the networks have the technical ca-
pacity to reach where they live. That problem is compounded
in rural areas, which are often too remote to make fast connections economical to provide to all residents. The absence
of home broadband connectivity is also a racial issue: His-
panic and African American students are significantly less
likely to have a broadband connection at home than Cauca-
sian or Asian American students.[13]

This problem of access is exacerbated by the push in
schools to encourage—and often require—students to use
the Internet as part of their schoolwork. A growing number

of states are requiring public school children to take an on-line course as part of their learning every year in high school. This push is driven by multiple forces. One is a well-meaning effort to provide twenty-first-century skills to students to prepare them to join a changing workforce. Critics of the push for twenty-first-century skills fear that these changes are driven by concerns about cost, a major force in school reform debates. Under budgetary pressure, schools are turning to low-cost options for providing access to certain courses that they cannot afford to offer by using live teach-ers. In other cases, individual teachers are requiring students to use the Internet to research term papers or create digital work-products. These are often sound and well-conceived assignments for kids as part of their various modes of learn-ing, and they make a great deal of pedagogical sense.[14]

Students who have good access to broadband Internet connections both at school and at home tend to have no problem completing such an assignment, whether it's a one-off requirement for a class or the work for a full-blown online course. Students in wealthy schools and districts have little to worry about in terms of accessibility and digital literacy. But in school districts with low-income populations, especially in rural areas, digital-era assignments can turn into a night-mare for students and their parents. If they don't have fast connections at home, students have to rush to try to get their work done during the school day or at after-school programs, though this strategy is often impractical. The small screens and slower transmission speeds of mobile devices over cellphone networks are inadequate for doing homework. These differences in Internet access point quality greatly affect student participation in online activities. The lower digital literacy rates found in areas with lower socioeconomic status simply compound the problem.[15]

Enter public libraries. Thanks to major national funding programs and advocacy by librarians, public libraries have played an essential function in meeting this need to provide children with fast Internet access outside of the school day and to improve their digital literacy. Over the past two decades, a combination of federal funding and a big push by the Bill and Melinda Gates Foundation has made fast Internet access in public libraries possible across America. Today 92 percent of the approximately 16,700 public libraries in the United States (or about 15,400 of them) offer wireless Internet access to their patrons. Every day schoolchildren across the country visit their public library, not to borrow a book or to talk to a reference librarian, but to connect to the Internet and complete their homework after school and before the library closes. Even after closing time, library parking lots are sometimes full of patrons sitting in their cars late into the night to take advantage of the free Wi-Fi that seeps outside of library walls.[16]

The enduring problem is that budget cuts have led libraries to reduce their hours and cut services at branches. Library hours of operation often overlap substantially with the school day, meaning that students who need the lifeline of free Internet access to complete their homework often have only a short window of time during which they can use the library. If they need to do research, writing, or digital production, this period can be too short for them to do a decent job of their homework. And demand frequently exceeds supply by a wide margin: earnest schoolchildren compete with job-seekers, game-players, the homeless, and all manner of other public library users for time on library terminals, a necessity in areas where most kids cannot afford their own laptop.[17]

The net result is that children and their parents migrate away from closed or crowded libraries to other places where they can get free Wi-Fi. For many American schoolchildren, this means a McDonald's or a Starbucks, which have longer hours, do not require a purchase of food to use the free Wi-Fi, and are within twenty miles of the homes of the vast majority of Americans. Between them, McDonald's and Starbucks have about 23,000 restaurants in America that offer free Wi-Fi—exceeding the total number of public libraries offering free Wi-Fi. Set aside concerns about healthy eating, growing rates of childhood obesity, and the long-term health care costs involved and focus on the problems this situation poses for learning alone. Not only are there no knowledgeable and helpful librarians at McDonald's and Starbucks restaurants, but the smells and sounds of a fryolator or a Frappuccino blender do not contribute to the best study environment.[18]

It seems obvious that our schoolchildren should not have to go to fast-food restaurants to finish their homework. Libraries would be a far better option. Students often report that they study at the library not only because of the free Internet access but also because of the quiet environment. In addition to being a more contemplative place, a library has helpful librarians who might provide a timely helping hand to a student struggling with a tricky problem. But hard budget choices—between books, staff salaries, utilities, and so forth—have forced the perverse outcome of kids leaving school and library environments to seek out commercial establishments that offer a means to get their homework done.[19]

The digital divide has another troubling dimension: the vast preparation gaps that separate our students. Researchers have shown what every schoolteacher knows: kids come to school with widely ranging abilities to learn the material and the skills expected of them. They have not only differences in access but differences in support structures and skills. These divides are not just about access; they go far deeper. These divides cannot be solved simply by improving the physical infrastructure. For example, in the one country in the world that can claim to have made the Internet as ubiquitous as electricity, the Netherlands, there are persistent differences in how effectively and productively youth from different socioeconomic backgrounds use the Internet. In the Netherlands, youth from lower socioeconomic groups use their access for entertainment at a greater rate than youth from higher socioeconomic groups. The opposite trend is observed for the use of access for information and scholarship.[20]

The problem of disparate digital expertise and practices between groups of students is not an achievement gap but a preparation gap. Rates of both achievement and preparation tend to correlate strongly to race and socioeconomic status, so much so that education levels are often used as a proxy by social scientists for wealth and status. So too for library usage: Pew's research shows that young people from lower-income backgrounds use libraries less frequently than those from higher-income backgrounds.[21]

In the digital era, these inequities are exacerbated. The young people who are most able to take advantage of digitally mediated forms of learning are often those with the highest socioeconomic status. The young people with the least support for avoiding the traps of the digital era—sharing too much information about oneself, getting into dangerous situations online, failing to distinguish credible from less credible information online—tend to come from the least-well-off families. As these twenty-first-century skills become more and more important, societies need affirmative strategies to head off growing inequalities.[22]

Libraries and talented librarians need to be at the center of strategies to lessen the preparation and skills gaps. Beyond providing broadband access, libraries have a critical role to play in supporting the digital literacy of any society. Teachers are often too stretched to meet the many expectations imposed on them by the prescribed curriculum and are left with little time to devote to digital education. But since schoolchildren are already coming to libraries in large numbers to use free Wi-Fi (and check out the occasional book), librarians have an important chance to help. Research shows clearly that any successful search for information, particularly in today's more complex information environment, depends on experience and guidance. Young children especially still rely on other people as a source of information. Savvy librarians can use the teaching moments that arise in a library—a student showing up with a personal interest in a subject or a hard problem assigned by a teacher—to help close these gaps in digital literacy. Librarians have an extraordinary opportunity today to build from strength: they are getting students in the door—as long as those doors are kept open and the lights turned on.[23]

CHILDREN ARE NOT the only patrons who continue to make extensive use of libraries. Adults matter to libraries too, of course, and they use them in vast numbers and for a wide array of purposes. Overall, usage of libraries has continued to be high across virtually all age groups. A major report on public libraries produced by the Institute of Museum and Library Services, a US government funding agency, showed that the nation's nearly 17,000 public libraries served 297.6 million people in 2010, out of a total population of 308.7 million. (From 2000 to 2010, the same report noted, state government funding for libraries fell 37.6 percent while federal government funding fell 19.3 percent. It seems extraordinary that a public service with such reach should be, in effect, punished despite its success by receiving a falling share of public resources.) More than half of all Americans use a public library regularly. In 2013 over half (54 percent) of Americans age sixteen or older said that they had visited a library in the previous twelve months.[24]

Adults tell researchers that they use libraries to borrow books, DVDs, CDs, materials for job-seeking, and materials related to becoming citizens, as well as to spend time with others in a public place. Circulation of materials is up across the board, from 43 million materials in 2002 to 69 million in 2011 in the libraries of the city of New York alone. Attendance at public events at libraries is also on the rise. In New York City, 17,000 programs in 2011 attracted more than 2.3 million attendees, a 40 percent increase since 2002.[25]

In addition to attracting large numbers of users, libraries have passionate supporters. The American Library Association hosts a web community called "I Love Libraries" that provides a venue for people to describe why they're passionate about libraries. The author Dennis Gaffney wrote: "I love libraries because they expect little but give much. They don't come with a curriculum and textbooks, but open stacks. There are no teachers to tell us what to read, just librarians who lie low unless asked for an opinion." Gaffney's sentiments are echoed by many others: libraries offer a low-key, accessible, usually open learning environment for people who are too old or too busy for school. Our democracies need libraries so that citizens can remain lifelong learners, no matter what their income or their access to formal education.

The independence and the public nature of libraries also appeal to patrons. Gaffney echoed the views of many when he argued, "I love libraries because their names have not yet been appropriated like those of sports arenas by the likes of Pepsi, Fleet Bank, or National Car Rental. The notion that anyone would name a community library the Tropicana Branch sounds absurd, and it should, because we own our libraries."

The independence of libraries matters because it means that our attention cannot be bought and sold in a library. We are free to pursue our own interests and ideas, without fear of reprisal or economic consequence. Our public spaces are under pressure from private interests, in real life and online. Libraries remain a powerful, appealing public space in communities all around the world.[26]

L IBRARIES THAT ARE properly supported and ambitiously led are pressing hard toward a sustainable, worthy future in which they will effectively serve their patrons of all ages. This time of change is a moment when libraries need to work together to build the future anticipated by many library users. If libraries don't meet the information needs of communities, then others will. Others are more likely to mix a profit motive in with activities that are broadly in the public interest, whether it's Amazon's interest in selling books, Google's interest in selling ads based on searches, or the interest at Starbucks and McDonald's in selling elaborate coffees and fast food. Libraries, not companies, should play the leading role as community meeting places built around ideas and dreams.

Finding ways to access information or entertainment will not be one of the primary challenges for library users in the future. Most information is already very accessible from most digital devices, and finding it is getting easier all the time. The mobile revolution—Internet-enabled tablets and phones in so many hands, coupled with growing Wi-Fi and cellular coverage—continues unabated each year. Much of the time, library users can access what they need from home or from the road. If one has the money, a book that's in print can be downloaded within seconds from several sources: via Amazon onto a Kindle, from Barnes & Noble onto a Nook, via a pile of for-profit services onto an iPad or an Android tablet, and so forth. Magazines, newspapers, recorded music, movies, television shows—all can be downloaded in moments to the same tablet, iPhone, or iPod through the Apple iTunes store or app store. Information is less scarce, and much more accessible, than it has been in the past.

Libraries may have a role to play in providing free access to these same digital services on networked devices, but that role is bound to be minor. There is certainly a public service involved in making sure that members of the public who cannot afford to pay for the newest, most recently copyrighted works can get access to them. It is plausible that libraries can help, at the margins, to mete out access to the latest bestselling novels or hit movies. But it makes no sense that in the future such a service would be provided by a geographically based, physical institution in each town. If all a library is doing is deciding who is first in line to download the latest James Patterson novel in a given zip code, there is no chance that communities will continue to employ humans, sitting in a bricks-and-mortar building in that zip code, to decide who gets access to the publicly funded version of that file for the next two weeks.

There is no question, however, that libraries offer much more than that. Library patrons—children and adults alike— realize this when they ask for help with a school project, attend a public lecture, learn about the citizenship process, cart home a stack of books on starting a new business, or simply read the newspaper or a picture book in a cool, quiet, safe space. Librarians build relationships with their patrons that provide meaning and value. These face-to-face interactions, in public spaces in communities, provide an essential service that is still worth paying for.

I have written much of this book sitting in libraries, public and academic, around the world. While working on a draft of this chapter, I happened to be in the Memorial Hall Library in downtown Andover, Massachusetts, where I now live. It is a wonderful town public library with helpful staff who are visible and accessible on the floor. People of all ages use the front room, which is filled with periodicals, best-sellers, and DVDs. A vibrant section of the main floor is frequented by schoolchildren, who flood in after the bells ring to set them free in the early afternoon. One afternoon I realized that all will be well in the world of libraries, at least for a while, when suddenly, above the usual sounds of the active library, I heard a thirteen-year-old shout into his iPhone, "Siri, what does 'terminal velocity' mean?" Siri—Apple's free, digital, and fairly unreliable virtual assistant—didn't seem to have a clue. I'm quite sure, however, that one of the nearby reference librarians could have easily helped the student find the answer.

Chapter Three

Spaces

The Connection Between the Virtual and the Physical

Create a hybrid space where analog and digital coexist.
—Jeffrey Schnapp, metaLAB (at) Harvard

O N MORE OR less any day during the academic year, if one were to walk through the reading room of the Harvard Law School library, one would find many of the seats occupied by students. These students are arrayed, side by side, at long tables, in a room with a high ceiling, beneath the steady gaze of legal giants from ages past (mostly white men, some in wigs). The students are most likely to gather in this great room to study the law, though not exclusively. Students from various fields around the university find their way to this inspiring space to do their research and to study for exams. On some days, a few professors sit among the students, perhaps in the same seats where they, too, once studied for exams as they were working toward their degrees.

Though they come from many walks of life and are of varying ages, the people toiling away in this particular library tend to have the same few objects in front of them on the long wooden tables. Coffee, kept in school-approved, oversized mugs with tight lids to protect the library and its books from spillage, is common. Nearly every student also has a laptop computer in front of her, connected to the library's wireless network. The laptop and the coffee might be what one would expect of studious young people of their generation.

But there is another common feature: almost to a one, law students have in front of them a heavy, bound, inches-thick legal casebook. These casebooks look very much like what law books have looked like for centuries. It is the familiar codex, essentially the same format that historical figures in law—luminaries by the names of Littleton, Coke, Blackstone, Story, and Holmes, the types of men whose portraits stare down upon the students in the reading room—used to publish their views. The physical, old-school casebook is an enduring feature of the study of law, even in our increasingly digital age.

Beside the casebook, these law students have a few other, smaller objects in front of them. Most of them have a ballpoint pen of some sort, along with a fat yellow highlighter. (Though I haven't conducted one, I'm entirely certain that an empirical study would show that sales of yellow highlighters are higher in law school bookstores than at comparable stores on other types of campuses.) The most diligent law students, poring over the same cases over and over again, saturate the pages of their casebooks with yellow ink. From time to time, they also underline the same point, for double-emphasis. And margins are often filled with notations in the students' handwriting, a running commentary on the holdings or dicta embedded in the opinions.[1]

These casebooks have survived the advent of the digital era for a reason: they are an effective way to convey information to students. They serve as useful canvasses on which students can work with the core material, the raw data, of legal information. But these casebooks are far from perfect. They are heavy and expensive, and they do not provide what digital formats will soon be able to offer in terms of interactivity, shared commentary, collective work spaces, and new connections between concepts.

Law students will probably still be lugging around massive casebooks a few years from now. For one thing, ebooks have yet to take hold among youth in general, though that tide may well be turning. For another, no one has designed a better law school casebook for the mass market of law students. But that will change. There are too many advantages to digital casebooks for this state of affairs to continue. Bound, legal casebooks, filled largely with public domain materials, at a cost of $150 each, will not survive the digital revolution. Students will migrate to better, cheaper, interactive textbooks for their legal study, accessed through iPad apps or web browsers on laptops.[2]

No matter how tempted libraries are to pin their hopes on the reassuring, studious scene at libraries like today's

Harvard Law School Library, the impending shift demands that librarians ask a series of hard questions. Why is it that students want to come to the *place* of a library to do their homework? What will happen if and when they are no longer using these cumbersome books? Could we do better, in a digital age, in terms of the materials that they are using to study? And if we were to take the physical books out of the equation, would the students leave the beautiful library spaces we painstakingly built and maintain for them, at great expense? If we cannot come up with positive answers to these questions, we stand to lose some of the last physical, public spaces that are not devoted to commercial pursuits.

A SUCCESSFUL LIBRARY SPACE supports library patrons as they make use of information in a variety of formats—no matter how the format or user access evolves in the coming years. Librarians—and the architects of libraries, for that matter—are grappling seriously with the connection between physical architecture and information architecture. One might infer that once the books are no longer in analog format, the need for library spaces will go away. That inference turns out to be wrong.

Imagine that the reading room of the Harvard Law School Library is now devoid of legal textbooks; gone, too, are the yellow highlighters and the black ballpoint pens. All that remains are the students, their laptops (perhaps replaced with smaller-format tablets, such as iPads), and their coffee (still in librarian-approved, covered travel mugs). Would these young people still line the long wooden tables of the library, day and night, as they do today?

They should—and probably will if librarians, and those of us who support them, are smart about this transition. Libraries provide services that have nothing to do with whether students are toiling away with physical books or digital versions of casebooks on iPads.

For one thing, most libraries provide essential contemplative spaces in the midst of an otherwise bustling, distracting world. The aura of a library reading room—whether designed for academics or for the public—is conducive to study. The primary function of the space is obvious: to read, reflect, write, and prepare for tests. Many students find that studying in their apartments or dorm rooms is less productive, in part because of associations with other activities, in part because of possible distractions. When one is in the library, one is there to study. (In theory anyway. Other, less scholarly uses of remote areas of library stacks, for instance, are well documented.)

In a digital era, spaces where people can come to study, read, and think are essential for communities and individuals to thrive. We already have too few such open, public spaces. Some libraries have experimented with digital-free zones, spaces where Wi-Fi and Ethernet do not reach, to allow the digital-era brain to disconnect from the network and its many distractions. Others have segmented spaces within their walls for a range of activities, some of which involve making noise (collaborative work) and others of which involve silent work (with librarians occasionally shushing a noisy interloper, as in days of yore). The contemplative spaces in libraries are well worth preserving, in part because they are lovely and in part because the always-on, highly connected pace of digital-era life can be overwhelming.

A second reason students might come to a library space, even if physical books are not part of the equation, is for the support and camaraderie that other humans provide. Studying, even on one's own, can feel like an inherently social activity. The long hours required to master the law of contracts, torts, or civil procedure in the first year of law school—or any other subject, for that matter—can go by more quickly for friends who are sharing the same experience, studying at one another's side, perhaps taking the same breaks to refill their coffee cups.

The other useful humans inhabiting library spaces, of course, are the librarians. Though recent studies confirm that students are less likely than they should be to consult a librarian in the course of research, that is no reason for libraries to give up on the essential service of reference support. Indeed, reference librarians can be even more useful in a digital age than they always were in the analog past.

With information about nearly any topic abundant, students are too likely to resort to the most immediate and easily accessible sources—those found through a Google search box or an iPhone. But these sources are often not the best. The most successful students are those who know that they can do better than grasp at the closest source of information.

Reference librarians, who spend their days learning what is available in a broad range of fields and how to search for it, provide a great service for students and other library patrons. In a world exploding with potential sources of information of widely varying quality and applicability, this core skill of librarians—as guides to the best resources—can be invaluable.

To date, librarians have been most effective when they are embedded in physical spaces, connected to ideas and to the act of knowledge transfer. Many libraries have experimented with virtual reference services. These remote services, which allow library patrons to chat with or email a librarian from anywhere, offer some promise, but they have not been wildly successful. Anyone, for instance, can log on to the Internet and consult a librarian from the San Francisco Public Library by chat or text at any hour when the actual library is open. Most academic libraries have put in chat services for their patrons to ask questions during operating hours, from wherever they might be.

These virtual services, though cool and appealing to some patrons, have not eliminated the need for staff reference librarians. Nor have the number of people using these virtual services come anywhere close to the number of people using physical reference services at most libraries. As it turns out, the most inventive of the experiments in virtual reference have been abandoned. The reference desks set up in Second Life, a virtual world that was briefly popular in the mid-2000s, have nearly all shut down. Many people, including students, still seem to like to step up to the actual reference desk to ask a live person for help rather than opening up a chat window. It bodes well for the future of physical libraries if this preference is explained by the simple appeal of the face-to-face, an important component of life that endures even in a digital era.

The simplest example of the enduring need for physical library space is that not all materials have yet been digitized. It's simply not true that you can find everything you need through a Google search. Many materials that are available in digital form are very expensive to obtain; when a library has a physical copy, it makes sense to provide that to a patron rather than to pay again for a digital copy. Students studying in their law texts online, for instance, will regularly need to consult texts that will not yet be easily available in digital formats. By studying in a library, they will be closer to the librarian, who can help them track down and gain access to this material more quickly—another plus for studying in the physical library rather than remaining in one's dorm room. Some of these advantages of physical library space will diminish as more and more material is available in digital formats, but considering that the digitization of all recorded knowledge is a gargantuan task, these advantages will not be disappearing anytime soon.

Moreover, at least in certain scholarly fields, the digital may never replace the physical as the best format for consulting materials. For instance, many of the important texts in art, architecture, and design are published in extremely large format. The images that are surrounded by text in published works are far larger than the screens that students typically use for their coursework, or that faculty members use for their research, for that matter. A physical library is required to select, obtain, store, and provide access to these large-format works.

And then there are the special collections. Historical materials, often brittle or otherwise too fragile to be safely handled repeatedly, must be stored with care by professional librarians and archivists. These materials can and should be digitized as soon as possible. The process of digitization can allow for a form of preservation as well as for greater access to materials that might not otherwise be consulted by students or researchers. But even after being digitized, the original physical materials still have substantial value. Scholars still raise grant money to travel long distances to consult the originals of works, even when high-resolution digital images are available to them from afar. Think of the glorious Beinecke Library at Yale, with its world-class curatorial staff to care for its historic collection in a striking, modern building in New Haven, Connecticut. Designed by the firm of Skidmore Owings and Merrill and completed in 1963, the Beinecke has translucent walls of Vermont marble and granite. This beautiful physical space would still be well worth a visit even if everything it contains, including an original Gutenberg Bible and Audubon's *Birds of America*, were visible online.

Historians of the book, an important and growing field, study the physical form of books as well as their contents. A digital facsimile would never be likely to do for their scholarly purposes. The smell of old books, the occasional drop of liquid on a page, the stitching at the center of an ancient manuscript, the ink of marginalia by an important commentator or reader of a work—each physical characteristic could have great and enduring value. For all these reasons, we need physical libraries, librarians, and archivists to keep doing most of what they are doing today in physical spaces.

Libraries, too, are shifting from places where information is used to places where information is created and shared. Librarians are at the center of making this shift happen. Kari Lämsä, the chief librarian at Helsinki's Library 10 and Meetingpoint/Urban Workshop, is one of the leading practitioners of a new kind of librarianship that takes advantage of this shift. "Libraries have always been places to use culture, use information," he said in an interview, but now, he added, a library is "a place to create information and culture." His patrons tell him they want to come to the library to make and record music and to learn about digital media. At Library 10, 80 percent of the events held are organized by patrons, not the staff. As chief librarian, Lämsä aspires to establish a co-working, co-creating atmosphere in which librarians and patrons frequently collaborate.

The team of librarians at Helsinki's Library 10 are pioneering another way to envision the role of the library: as an "information gas station." The two self-service "data pumps" come with a promise to answer any question the library's "gas station" customer might ask, within reason. A library employee is on hand to help. People have asked for recipes for a chocolate cake, information on the flight paths of flies, and an intelligible explanation of Einstein's theory of relativity. The aim of the information gas station concept, merely a pilot experiment rather than a full-blown library, is to bring the world's information networks within the reach of all citizens. The information kiosk is mobile. It can be located wherever people might be around the city, whether in post offices, aquatic centers, or trade fairs. Customers can request the information they are looking for over the Internet or by phone or text message, and questions are also answered once a week on the radio. Human beings—librarians—are still central to the equation. The powerful core idea is to focus less on books per se and more on knowledge transfer within a community.

When Kari Lämsä asked fellow librarians why they enjoyed working closely with young patrons, they told him: "Because children think it's fun." Whether as "information gas stations," "maker-spaces," or classic reading rooms, libraries can definitely be fun. Librarians like Lämsä and his collaborators are leading the way.

JUST AS THERE is no single "library user experience" today, there is no single type of library space that is needed for the digital-plus age. There hasn't been one single type for centuries, at least not since the handful of libraries of antiquity served a tiny community of nobles and those for whom they provided patronage. The experience of a law student or a historian of the book may seem rarified. Academic libraries, archives, and special collections, after all, make up a small proportion of the overall world of libraries. The use of these lovely spaces by the lucky few hardly makes the case for the public and school libraries that make up the mass of libraries in the United States and around the world.

Those who grew up in a town with a Carnegie library have enjoyed the closest thing to a "common" library experience in the United States. A central tenet of Carnegie's philanthropic system was the provision of a standardized design and set of expectations for towns accepting his gift of a library. The net effect of Carnegie's gift was an explosion of public library construction according to a classical design of what a library should be, and now the Carnegie library, set in a town center overlooking a green, plays an outsized role in our collective imagination of what a library is. In fact, however, there are actual Carnegie libraries in fewer than 1,500 communities across the country. Variety turns out to be the norm when it comes to libraries, not uniformity.

Public libraries today serve a growing range of functions, for a broad range of people, and their services usually expand far beyond providing easy access to printed books. The foot traffic in libraries today confirms this basic fact about libraries. The three large New York City library systems, for instance, which boast more than two hundred branches citywide, have over the last decade seen a 40 percent increase in the number of people attending programs, such as computer literacy classes and workshops on entrepreneurship. Urban public libraries meet many of the needs of the past—such as providing a safe, cool place for children in the summertime—while dreaming up new ways to draw people through their doors.[3]

Innovation in library services is cropping up all over the United States and all around the world. Libraries check out everything from bicycles to therapy dogs to help students relax during exam times. Students at the Yale Law School can check out the lovable twelve-year-old therapy dog Monty for fifteen- to twenty-minute sessions of relaxation, alone or with a small group of friends. Libraries in the Midwest have created programs to teach people how to develop new skills, including how to carve a pig. The lure of do-it-yourself bacon production is bringing people into libraries in meaningful numbers, even if it does leave a bit of a mess—and has very little to do with lending bound books. Librarians today are nothing if not creative in finding ways to serve their communities.[4]

The most creative libraries are pulling people who are not yet using libraries into attractive physical spaces—rather than leaving this job to commercial establishments. If these emergent forms of informal learning continue to grow in importance, there is a real opportunity for libraries to play an important role in designing common spaces for the future, either in lieu of the private companies that dominate them now or perhaps in partnership with them.

For some libraries, the approach is obvious: if children, and especially boys, are using library computers anyway to play games, channel this interest productively by introducing well-structured game environments into the physical library itself. The YouMedia movement is creating appealing spaces inside public libraries for young people to participate in making new knowledge, alongside their peers and mentors. The first YouMedia center, based in the Chicago Public Library's main building, offers young people a casual, well-wired space for what Mizuko Ito, a scholar at the University of California–Irvine, calls "hanging out and geeking around." The programs offered through YouMedia teach children digital literacy and production skills and how to create new knowledge in interactive formats, publish online in multimedia, and parse credible from less credible information in digital formats. Thanks to the leadership of academics, forward-looking youth librarians and funders such as Connie Yowell at the MacArthur Foundation and Jorge Martinez at the Knight Foundation, YouMedia centers are popping up in libraries around the country. Other initiatives to develop "hacker" and "maker" spaces in libraries are offering similarly innovative programming.[5]

Programs centered on gaming are a piece of what is bringing kids in large numbers into public libraries around the country. These projects are active at big-city libraries and small-town, Carnegie-style libraries alike. At the Chicago Public Library, the YouMedia center supports a student group that plays and reflects on their love of gaming. The kids have developed and keep up a website called The Library of Games, where they create podcasts, write blog posts, and publish reviews of video games. The redesign of the

Boston Public Library's Johnson building includes a gaming and video room as part of the new "teen central" area. Other libraries, like the small-town Dover Public Library in the suburbs of Boston, offer services for teens that include test prep for the SAT alongside video gaming stations in the children's section and running commentary about games on their websites.[6]

These programs are so successful and popular among young people because educators and librarians are encouraging learners to follow their interests, in both digital and physical environments. It is not necessary to change the entire paradigm of education, nor to throw out the entire list of skills and subject matter that our schools cover today. The point is instead to make something of the advantages that informal types of learning, mediated by technology, can offer. Kids are learning on their mobile devices, for instance. Consider the amount of algebra a student can learn from a clever video game called DragonBox, which steps a student through new tools and skills as they solve increasingly complex equations. Kids are able to spend hours per day playing games because games hold their attention. Libraries should find ways to provide kids with applications that are useful and ever-present on their smartphones. Teaching programs that have the orientation of games—quests to be completed, levels to be attained, levels of mastery to wear as badges—can engage children who are otherwise less inclined to study.[7]

Even in informal learning environments, kids still need the support of adults. Librarians, like all teachers, can be brokers of learning experiences, helping to match student interests to available options. ("You like computers? Maybe you'd like to try Scratch, where you learn to make your own programs.") In places like the YouMedia center, adults are needed to serve as translators to help students understand what they are learning and provide context. Meredith Johnson, a reference librarian at the Johnson County Central Resource Library in Kansas, teaches an introductory MakerBot class for those who want to learn to use a 3-D printer. Johnson herself was self-taught; she had never used a 3-D printer before it showed up in her library's maker-space. The uses of a 3-D printer in a library are impossible to predict and often wonderful to behold. One of the products developed in the library's maker-space was a prosthetic hand. A disabled boy, nine-year-old Matthew, worked with a sixteen-year-old family friend to create his own "Robohand." Instead of spending $18,000 on a commercial prosthetic product, Matthew custom-made his own new brightly colored hand, with help from his local librarians and his own family network.[8]

Libraries should continue to build these maker-spaces, where young people (and older people, for that matter) can learn to build out into the emerging digital environment. Programs such as YouMedia bring librarians into close and promising contact with young people at just the moments when kids are open to connecting with others. They provide essential pathways for mentorship between young people and adults. Librarians will also no doubt learn from the kids they are working with—about their information habits (both good and bad) and about how to offer other useful digital-era services. In the process, librarians and their patrons will be building an open, innovative digital future together.

These kinds of mentoring and teaching practices often require replacing traditional library spaces with interactive environments, but they are smart and necessary. Some prominent researchers, like UC-Irvine's Mizuko Ito, see them as essential to the ability of young people to adapt to learning in the twenty-first century. Much turns on how programming and physical layouts are designed to lead to positive learning outcomes for the kids who show up at libraries, but these innovative approaches to librarianship should not be controversial.

A very real challenge, however, is ensuring that people keep coming to physical libraries even when mobile access is ubiquitous. Librarians well know that the discovery of information is moving out of physical locations and into distributed spaces. Discovery now happens wherever a library patron happens to be. Smartphones with apps and web browsers or small tablets with network connections are increasingly the means of discovering information and knowledge. The results are instantaneous. People with an Internet connection on their mobile device—a growing population, not just in the United States but globally—can do what they once did at the library in interstitial moments, anywhere and anytime a network connection is close by. This shift away from place-based access toward mobile access to information technology is just as important for libraries as the shift to digital from analog and from the stand-alone to the networked. But with classes on computer literacy and offerings like maker-spaces, libraries are successfully drawing in people of all ages and making it clear that libraries are more than just places to discover and obtain copies of recorded knowledge.

A LTHOUGH LIBRARIES NEED to create new and innovative programs, that will not be sufficient to secure a bright future for libraries. As libraries find new ways to bring people through their doors, they must resist becoming just community centers. There is no question that community centers are wonderful, and they play an important role in many cities and towns. But if libraries are nothing more than community centers, then we will have community centers in every town, but not libraries. In some towns, classic public libraries have been closed and reopened to meet a broad range of other purposes, including bed-and-breakfasts. A community center is much cheaper and easier to run than a public library. And a community center lacks the inspired, essential human beings that help make sense of the knowledge around us: trained librarians.[9]

Libraries can avoid this fate by ensuring that they function as both cultural and learning environments. However, they must navigate away from two dangerous ends of a spectrum. At one end, libraries cannot just be places to get information, given that people think they can find other ways to get information. At the other end, libraries cannot merely provide services that can be delivered in any public space by any capable, creative event organizer.[10]

The sweet spot for libraries will be where the physical and the digital—where fun and learning—come together, as Library 10 in Helsinki, the Johnson County Central Resource Library in Kansas, and the YouMedia centers are demonstrating. Neither the analog nor the digital alone is sufficient in cultural and intellectual life. People are moving away from physical objects, by and large, as sources of discovery and information. But the need for human interaction—for humanity, in the broadest sense—has never been greater. Libraries can thrive at precisely this intersection.[11]

The spatial model for libraries in a digital era should be closer to educational institutions than to community centers. In many cases, libraries function as the "second chance" public school for those who either didn't or couldn't take advantage of their schooling. For some kids, the public library is a refuge and a learning space while they are still in school. For others, the public library offers a way to gain skills that they didn't happen to get while they were in school or that they need to transition to new careers. Job readiness programs, such as the youth-oriented initiative at the public library in Far Rockaway, New York, offer an essential service to teens that they don't get elsewhere. Libraries that offer intensive literacy and pre-GED courses report strong participation among job seekers. For older library users, a library is a vibrant "third place" away from a home that may seem lonely or a senior center that may lack pizzazz. Libraries provide a space for senior citizens to read periodicals they can't afford on their own, socialize with other readers, learn about computer literacy, and master the intricacies of free online tax filing—all social, cultural, and learning experiences.

Libraries play a special role as spaces in the lives of people who come to a new country. In the United States, libraries are the institutions most trusted by recent immigrants. For these new residents, the public library system may make up for the schooling they didn't get in their home country, and it may also provide the first friends in their new country and an on-ramp into the new culture. New immigrants use libraries as a means to learn the local language and to prepare for citizenship. For all these reasons, a library should look more like a learning environment than a totally flexible, all-purpose space. The design of a library should build from this position of strength. Libraries should evoke the power of learning and inspire the production of new knowledge.[12]

Librarians and architects should work together to envision what spaces should look like to meet the cultural, social, and information needs of specific communities in a digital-plus era. Academic, public, and school libraries have distinctive needs, and a single library type for them is no more likely to be appropriate now than in the past. In every case, however, libraries need to offer some spaces that are quiet and contemplative and others that are bustling and exciting. Libraries provide context and assurance for people who feel confused, as they often do, when coping with ubiquitous, and yet insufficient, information. Libraries provide points of access for both digital and physical materials for those who cannot afford to pay for it on their own. What that means for libraries will vary from place to place, from population to population, but it will not be captured in a space that looks like an anodyne community center. Libraries, as spaces, need to continue to inspire the public to dream big and to think great thoughts. Cities, towns, and academic communities of all shapes and sizes need the free, open public spaces that libraries—and only libraries—provide.

Chapter Four

Platforms

What Cloud Computing Means for Libraries

*There are perhaps no days of our childhood we lived
so fully as those . . . we spent with a favorite book.*
—Marcel Proust, *On Reading* (1906)

M Y EIGHT-YEAR-OLD daughter was on a reading binge.
She was cruising through several books a day. These
books were all part of different series that appealed to girls of
her age. The books about the Warrior Cats were a huge hit.
Nine books about the Sisters Grimm held her attention for
a while. The series about the Boxcar Children had a similar
grip on her. She read every one of the Encyclopedia Brown
mysteries about a boy detective, just as her older brother had
before her. The seven Harry Potter novels brought months of
enjoyment, every one of them read and reread.

One of the series that grabbed my daughter's attention
most effectively told the stories of American Girl dolls. These

narratives are all set in different historical contexts. One book is about Kaya, a member of the Nez Perce tribe, in the eighteenth century. Another is about Josefina, who lives in New Mexico in the nineteenth century. The protagonist of a third is Kit, who uses her wits to survive life as a young girl during the Great Depression. The books take young readers through American history as seen by fictional girls. There are as many as six books for every doll.

The good news for our family budget: the local town public library had several books in each of these series. We'd haul book bags full of them home from the library, and my daughter would plow her way through them. The less good budget news (though excellent news from a learning perspective): neither we nor the collections at the town's public library or independent bookseller could fully keep up with her pace.

As I watched her with these books, it dawned on me that my daughter was agnostic as to whether the text was printed or presented to her in digital form. She was happy either way: the format was immaterial to her speed or enjoyment. She just wanted to read them. (She did express one format-related preference: reading in the cloud-based Amazon Kindle service was less good than reading on the app-based Amazon Kindle service on my iPad. It was easier, she said, to turn the pages in the app than in the web browser. Fair enough.)

One night during her American Girl reading binge, I was working late at home. Our son was watching a movie (licensed, incidentally, as a short-term rental and running not on a TV but from Amazon's streaming video service on a MacBook Pro laptop in another room). Our daughter had run out of books from the library. Something new had grabbed her attention: American Girls had released a new doll, named Saige (the "Girl of the Year" for 2013), along with several books about her. My daughter had learned about Saige and gotten hooked on the books when she was in the online world associated with the dolls.

The company's strategy for connecting the physical and the virtual is extremely clever and, in its way, instructive. When a child opens her American Girl doll gift box, she finds inside a free pass to a companion website, called Innerstar University, or InnerstarU. The girl pesters her parents for help logging in to a virtual world where she can create an avatar, or digital character, based on the physical form of the doll she is holding in her arms. She navigates her avatar around a stylized, online college campus, answering questions to earn points. By many accounts, it's clear that kids (and adults too) love collecting "points" in virtual environments, regardless of whether those points ever amount to much.[1]

Once my daughter is logged in to InnerstarU, she finds quickly that one of the primary venues on campus is the library, where the avatar has to answer clever questions that might otherwise appear on a worksheet in a second-grade science or social studies classroom. If she gets stuck, she can ask for help at the virtual reference desk. Visitors to the site can sign up their real-life friends as friends in this virtual campus world and chat back and forth.

I had noticed that these programs manage to hold the attention of girls for hours on end. The students are learning something through the questions, no doubt. They are prompted to ask their parents questions about online safety ("Should I make friends with that person, Daddy?"), and they learn good general practices for research, such as going to a reference desk for help when stumped.

That evening, my daughter "checked out" the first chapter of the latest American Girl book (Saige) from the InnerstarU virtual library. She then asked me if we could buy a copy of the full text from Amazon, which she'd already found online, and download it to the Kindle app on my iPad. I said sure. An hour or so later, she'd read it entirely. I was still working, and the movie was still going in the other room. I bought her another book for the Kindle. And then, an hour later, a third, all part of the same series. I had told her that I believe in buying books, and she was holding me to my word. The only thing that saved me from buying even more books (at $5.69 a pop) was the arrival of her bedtime.

This experience got me thinking. There may be a future in which the library (as well as the physical bookstore, by the way) is bypassed, more or less altogether. There are several possible futures, none of them particularly attractive for libraries, for authors and publishers, for bookstore owners, for readers, or for our democracy—for various reasons. In one version of the future, the discovery of what to read and the discussion of the material both move online, but libraries remain places of fulfillment (where you go to get the texts, at least as an option) and shared public spaces. That world is not a terrible one. Libraries could survive such a change.

In a scarier version of the future, libraries get cut out of the process altogether and are rendered obsolete. If Amazon, Apple, Google, and the American Girl company become not just the discovery mechanisms but also the primary providers of recorded entertainment—the books my daughter wants to read, the movies my son wants to watch, probably all the music they want to listen to—what place will be left for libraries? And will there be a public option of any sort—a way to get these materials free of charge, whether in printed form or downloaded to a device?

Those who care about the future of libraries need to stand and fight for the importance of a public option. There will no doubt continue to be a role for for-profit companies in the process of publishing, discovering, sharing, discussing, and buying books and other forms of recorded entertainment. Publishers, for instance, make a profit as they select which books will find their way into the mainstream. Along the way, publishers and the editors they employ improve the quality of the books they have decided to publish through professional editing, formatting, indexing, and so forth. The marketing mechanism of publishers helps books find receptive audiences. These functions are important.

But there must also be a public option in the digital age. Librarians help match people up with knowledge and information that are free to all, without the bias in favor of certain information that a for-profit inevitably brings to the task.

So far, as libraries have adjusted to the digital era, the rate of change in institutions that serve the public has been outstripped by the rate of change in for-profits—not least because the effective rate of federal and local funding has fallen off. The risk to libraries and the reading public posed by this asymmetry is a kind of enclosure movement of our cultural and scientific heritage.

The most successful online "learning" environment in which my daughter has found herself was created by a doll company, not by a public library. There is no public library that I (or my daughter, for that matter) have encountered that has been as effective at merging the physical and the digital as the American Girl company. Likewise, many adults remark on the importance of Google's search function or Amazon's recommended book service, in contrast to what they encounter at their local library.[2]

The risk of a small number of technically savvy, for-profit companies determining the bulk of what we read and how we read it is enormous. The great beauty of the rich, diverse library system that has developed over the past century and a half has been the role of librarians in selecting and making available a range of materials for people to consult and enjoy. No one pressing an ideology can co-opt this system; no single commercial entity can do an end run around the library system in the interest of profit. Scholars can rely on major research libraries to collect broadly and evenly across disciplines. Towns, cities, and states can rely on historical societies and archives to maintain records of the past. And every community can rely on its public library to offer a culturally relevant, broad-based collection of materials that can be consulted for free. Both those in the public sector and those in the private sector need to double down on our investment in the library system to make it competitive with the well-funded, innovative technology companies that increasingly dominate the information landscape. And librarians need to do their part by adapting their practices to address this peril.

"Cooperation is an unnatural act" for libraries and librarians, says David Ferriero, the Archivist of the United States. Cooperation, despite its difficulty, is essential to the future of libraries. Mr. Ferriero is an expert practitioner of this unnatural act. As a library director in universities and in the public library world, he figured out ways to partner with other libraries in the service of his immediate patrons and the field at large. As President Barack Obama's appointee to the job of our nation's archivist—he occasionally signs his emails AOTUS, a play on the presidential moniker POTUS (President Of The United States)—Ferriero has championed federal agencies working together to digitize public materials and get them into the hands of those who want to access them. But even for such a powerful and well-regarded leader, getting other institutions in the library, archival, and museum worlds to play together nicely is hard.[3]

Libraries do not have a choice but to work together to build a common, digital infrastructure. Collaboration sounds obvious, and it may seem easy enough, but it requires a major shift in the way libraries understand their roles. For centuries, libraries have remained essentially separate, even competing with one another to establish and maintain the greatest collection. There have been tentative efforts at cooperation in the form of collecting agreements and library consortia, but now a new level of cooperation is essential if libraries are to remain places of fulfillment and crucial public spaces. The initial locus of activity has moved from the immediate and the place-based to the network, and before long readers of all ages will prefer digital materials to print and will use collections that reside in "the cloud"—the jargon-y term for shared storage and computing power online.[4]

Libraries need to recast themselves as platforms rather than as storehouses. By "platform" I am referring to the easy, effective access to information and knowledge that libraries provide. A platform can certainly be a place—say, Ferriero's National Archives and all the presidential libraries he supports, as well as the "information gas stations" cropping up in Europe—and it can also be a service. The key is to establish a series of nodes in a larger network, staffed by thoughtful people who can help their patrons make the most of what is connected to that network. The crucial elements of the library as platform are the access to information that libraries offer, the expert advice in navigating through the information environment, and the connections to larger networks.

The library as platform contrasts with the traditional library as storehouse—a place where physical objects are stored for later retrieval. As a platform, a library brings people together with powerful ideas, whether in physical or virtual form, whether recorded or live. The people who work at the library see themselves as managing and supporting this platform. They do so not on their own as a free-standing institution, but embedded in the large and growing network of libraries also functioning as platforms. Many libraries are successfully making the switch to functioning as a platform— as a hybrid that exists at once in both physical and virtual environments.[5]

The biggest structural change that will occur in libraries in the next ten years has to do with the storage of information. Two powerful forces are working in the same direction: the percentage of people reading ebooks or otherwise encountering digital rather than analog objects, and the benefits of cloud computing. As people's use of information is increasingly mediated by digital technologies, the function and practice of libraries will continue to change. Instead of storing redundant sets of physical materials, libraries will begin to share access to commonly held digital materials. To the chagrin of many today, libraries will also be in the business of leasing access to materials rather than owning copies of what they lend out.

These inexorable moves toward the digital, networked, mobile, and cloud-based library are substantial and happening quickly. But these changes are not happening in one fell swoop, and they must be well coordinated. One of the biggest challenges of running a library today is determining how quickly to make the move in this new digital direction. The way in which things are moving seems clear, but not all library users are digitally savvy and not all of them prefer digital materials. Many of the people libraries serve today are ill equipped to take advantage of all the great things about the digital present and future. Since libraries must be guided by those they serve, they will be awkwardly straddling the analog and the digital for some period of time. Libraries and their partners in archives, museums, and funding agencies ought to work together to create common cloud-based infrastructure as well as materials and code. Libraries don't have to make this switch on their own, one at a time, and in fact there are good reasons why they should not.

The library community should learn from how the Internet and the web have been built up over the past several decades. No one information architect dreamed up the Internet and started building it. The Internet was built over time, through massive coordination across public and private lines. Much of the early funding came from the government, especially the Department of Defense. Many of the early insights came out of the academic sector, particularly computer scientists who wanted to establish new communication mechanisms and protocols. Much of what has happened since has been built out by the private sector, in ways that have both generated massive profits for investors and shareholders and served the greater good, by and large. The Internet is not perfect; nor is the way it came about perfect. But it has scaled incredibly well and thrown off a great deal of innovation—both of which libraries urgently need to do as well.

Although individuals and particular institutions played essential roles in designing and building the Internet and the web, the key institutions in its growth have been highly decentralized and inventive in their mode of governance. There was no big building, with large conference tables around which sage men and women designed a new system and then commissioned people to build it. Especially in the early days of the 1960s, 1970s, and 1980s, there was instead a motley assortment of brilliant, imaginative people working more or less in loose coordination with one another toward a common goal. A few individuals played outsized roles, to be sure. Often bearded white guys in sandals, they are brilliant scientists and the pioneers of the digital era: Vint Cerf and his colleagues early on; Sir Tim Berners-Lee at CERN, who invented the web, and his peers at MIT; Jon Postel and his friends, who dreamed up and managed important naming conventions; and so forth. But the institutions that managed the development of key aspects of the digital revolution were lightly coordinated, largely informal bodies like the Internet Engineering Task Force (IETF) and the World Wide Web Consortium (W3C). Since then, the open-source and open-access worlds have shown what similar organizations—such as the Free Software Foundation, the Mozilla Foundation, and the Wikimedia Foundation—can build on these open protocols and systems.

Librarians, in a handful of important cases, have employed similar models. These experimental approaches point the way forward for libraries as collaborators. The Mellon

Foundation, for instance, has funded work by the Council on Library and Information Resources (CLIR) to build open-source collection management tools. Librarians have teamed up with Wikipedians to improve the quality of Wikipedia articles and associated metadata. Giants of the open-source and open-access worlds, like Brewster Kahle, have built large-scale digital library systems, such as the Internet Archive.

One of the most extensive coordinated efforts to recast libraries as platforms, the initiative to build the Digital Public Library of America, is well under way. Its goal is to establish a national library platform for the United States—and in some respects for the whole world—in the digital age. The building of a digital public library began with agreement on a broad vision. In October 2010, about forty leaders from libraries, foundations, academia, and technology agreed to work together to create "an open, distributed network of comprehensive online resources that would draw on the nation's living heritage from libraries, universities, archives, and museums in order to educate, inform, and empower everyone in the current and future generations." I was among those who agreed to work toward this common goal.[6]

During a two-year planning process, we crisscrossed America and solicited widely diverse views on how to build this platform. The process took the form of a national design charrette that engaged more than 1,000 people, online and in person, at dozens of meetings between 2010 and 2012. The process was extensive on purpose: the idea has been to ensure that we are building toward a truly international resource that will serve as many people and libraries as possible. The design process and the decisions made along the way have been carefully documented online on the project's website, wiki, and multiple listservs.[7]

In April 2013, we were set to launch the first beta version of the DPLA at the Boston Public Library. The system had come in on time and on budget, and we were excited about the splash that the kickoff would make. The BPL was a carefully chosen venue. The first municipally funded public library in America, the BPL's historic McKim building is an icon in the world of libraries.

The launch didn't happen. The very week we were scheduled to unveil the DPLA, bombs exploded on the sidewalk outside the Boston Public Library, steps from where we planned to launch. It seemed implausible to host a major celebration in the immediate wake of the deadly Boston Marathon bombings of April 15. So we launched the DPLA virtually instead. As sad as the story was on so many levels, there seemed to be something fitting about a virtual launch of a digital public library system for the country. Virtual launches took place in multiple locations that day, including at the New York Public Library. An early partner in this effort, the NYPL today has more than 1 million digitized objects accessible through the DPLA.

The first iteration of the DPLA is very simple. It is grounded in the fundamental library principle of "free to all," only designed as a digital platform rather than as a bricks-and-mortar library. It combines a group of rich, interesting digital collections from state and regional digital archives with the special collections of major university libraries and federal collections. The DPLA is growing, at Internet scale and speed, to include collections from every corner of the nation. It is built to demonstrate how powerful and exciting it can be to bring together America's digitized materials, metadata (including catalog records, for instance), code, and tools into an open, shared resource.

The DPLA is a platform for libraries. Much like the Internet itself, it operates on the network model. The DPLA is the central nexus for a growing series of "hubs": organizations throughout the country that provide digital material for the public and services to other libraries and are seeking to digitize their holdings and make them broadly available. The DPLA's first fifteen hubs span the United States, providing a geographically and historically diverse look at our nation's archives. These first hubs include the Mountain West Digital Library (Utah, Nevada, and Arizona), Digital Commonwealth (Massachusetts), the Digital Library of Georgia, the Kentucky Digital Library, the Minnesota Digital Library, the South Carolina Digital Library, and the Oregon Digital Library. Each of these organizations in turn assists local and regional libraries, museums, and archives in digitizing and sharing materials online. Since then, many other states have joined, including New York and Connecticut. The goal is for every one of the fifty states to be connected before long through digital on-ramps to this national system.[8]

The DPLA's hubs each contain unique, valuable materials. The Minnesota Digital Library, for instance, hosts resources from more than 150 cultural institutions state-wide at its Minnesota Reflections site. Contributors to the collection range from the Minnesota Streetcar Museum to the US Army Corps of Engineers in St. Paul. This digital collection, now more than ten years old, includes maps, images, and documents pertinent to local historical research and to any comprehensive exploration of the state's history and geography. The Mountain West Digital Library, meanwhile, contains the Western Soundscape Archive, a collection from the University of Utah of nearly 3,000 sound clips recorded from the landscape and natural environment of the Mountain West region. Ever wonder what a Wyoming toad sounds like? There's a recording online, and you can find it through the DPLA from any mobile device or home computer.[9]

In addition to the state-based hubs, the DPLA brings together content from major institutional digital collections. The special collections of Harvard University, the DPLA's first university-based hub, for instance, include many of the digitized papers of Emily Dickinson. The National Archives includes the original copy of the Declaration of Independence and millions of other fascinating objects. Through the DPLA, you can find rare moving images of how US soldiers prepared and fired artillery rounds deep into German military operations in Verdun, France, in 1918, courtesy of the National Archives. The Smithsonian Institution and many other major collections are also making contributions from their holdings to ensure that digital scanning efforts, in both the private and public sectors, pay dividends for libraries of all kinds and for their patrons. The digital aggregation of these materials will make it much easier for library patrons to find them. This concerted effort to aggregate and improve metadata will bring resources to the surface of web searches, revealing highly useful information that might otherwise have remained buried.

The structure of the DPLA hubs offers a preview of what a platform approach to libraries can accomplish on a national level. Each of the service hubs, which can be run by state librarians, big public libraries, academic research centers, or others, collects content from its region and assists the smaller libraries and archives responsible for that content in the process. The DPLA aggregates the materials and in turn connects users to the content across these many regional and institutional digital libraries. In much the same way that you might find a book not available at your local library through an interlibrary loan system, the DPLA links digital collections from across the United States to make a wide variety of content directly available to users. Because this approach is built for the size and scope of the vast network of American cultural heritage institutions, it can and does scale. After a year of operations, and with only a tiny staff, the DPLA has gone from zero to 7.5 million curated objects in its database.

If the library-as-platform approach works, the DPLA will not serve as a destination site itself—not primarily anyway. Yes, anyone today can go directly to http://dp.la on their mobile device or computer and look something up, as they might in Google or Bing. But most people, most of the time, will access DPLA-related materials through their local cultural heritage institution—a local public library, for instance, or a historical society, archive, museum, or college library. The idea is to allow universal access to materials in the DPLA to the greatest extent possible. The DPLA makes its code and services available for free, on an open-source basis. This openness means that anyone—whether a nonprofit or a for-profit, an individual or a big library—can build innovative new applications on this new platform. Through its network of service hubs, the DPLA also supports the digitization of records, the creation of metadata, and the long-term preservation of our cultural record.

Within a year of going live, the DPLA has already been accessed millions of times. A wide array of people have been using it. Many of the enthusiastic early customers are school-children and their teachers. Eighth-graders used the DPLA to complete a research project on the 1920s in the United States, drawing on audio and video recordings to enhance their projects. A sixth-grade class read *The Watsons Go to Birmingham* and used the DPLA to research the civil rights movement. A high school sophomore relied on the DPLA for a presentation on the "Bread and Roses" strike. On the first day it went live, a graduate student tweeted that he had found a new primary source in the DPLA to support his dissertation. In each case, these users gained access to a nationally scaled library with carefully curated materials—from a web browser.

The DPLA is intended to encourage the active participation of citizens. In addition to providing a way to access information from around the country, the DPLA also enables people to contribute information to the national database. Imagine someone who wishes to digitize a series of historically significant photographs found in a trunk in her basement. Today she can take the photographs to her local historical society, and if she lives in one of the states that has an on-ramp to the DPLA, a historical society employee can help her digitize her entire collection, then use an app he found through the DPLA to curate the collection online. Although this person might have no previous experience using a computer, she is able to contribute to the expansion of knowledge about her town's history online. Meanwhile, scanning initiatives by regional organizations like the DPLA's service hubs provide the physical equipment for smaller, local institutions to digitize their own histories.

One of the key functions of the DPLA is to serve as an on-ramp for local and regional organizations to move into the digital realm. Many libraries and local historical societies do not yet have the skills and systems in-house to take advantage of the possibilities of digital librarianship. The DPLA is a mechanism for both librarians and library users to access and contribute materials in their possession to a national data store, while building essential digital skills. Before too long, the DPLA staff anticipate being able to commission mobile scanning units—"Scannebagos," or Winnebagos with scanners in the back, staffed by helpful librarians and archivists (or perhaps Airstreams if the Winnebago company doesn't wish to partner with us)—to drive across the country and help get our cultural history digitized and made available. By driving through America, the DPLA community could bring alive our cultural heritage in ways that have never before been possible. The results of these tours would be immediately available to anyone, from anywhere in the world, through the DPLA platform.[10]

Here is the key point about the DPLA: the DPLA will be what we, the people, decide to make it, as a shared, public-spirited resource, not what a for-profit firm thinks the future of libraries should look like. Already, the DPLA is a place for people to go to find useful and fascinating digital materials online and a radically open platform that makes a lot of exciting material available more broadly. It also provides a lot of code and services that technologists can do interesting things with. An example is the integration of the DPLA into the Wikipedia platform, which has combined a large open digital library with the largest encyclopedia in the world. Over time, the DPLA will grow into a platform that serves libraries, archives, and museums and all those who rely on them.

The Digital Public Library of America has its critics. One counterargument is that investments in digital infrastructures at scale will undermine support for the traditional and the local. As the chairman of the DPLA, I hear this critique in the question-and-answer period of nearly every presentation I give. The concern is not that the DPLA is a bad idea. In fact, virtually all of the librarians (and ordinary citizens too) I've spoken with in five years of barnstorming for the DPLA agree that it is a great idea; many have joined hands and are helping to build it. The concern is that support for the DPLA will undercut already eroding support for small, local public libraries. I am deeply sympathetic to this concern—nothing would be a more perverse outcome of a well-intended initiative.

While the argument that common investment in a large-scale digital platform will erode local support is enough to give sufficient pause, it misses the larger point. No matter how successful the DPLA may be, local libraries will always continue to serve as essential access points and the stewards of physical materials. There is no chance that the Harvard Law Library will shut down and dismiss its many talented librarians once all the recorded law of every land can be found online. YouMedia centers haven't put the city libraries of Chicago and Miami out of business. A successful DPLA offers so much information that the need for a local librarian as curator and guide, far from disappearing, will in fact grow. The larger point that this counterargument may overlook is that libraries need to develop a shared, common, and public infrastructure for the future of libraries—or someone else will, most likely driven by the profit motive. Amazon and Google are already, in their way, doing so. The providers of ebook platforms are likewise creating this infrastructure. The cloud itself, which will host most digital content moving forward, is built and maintained exclusively by private players.

The DPLA and other coordinated efforts to reconceive libraries as platforms are already offering promising alternatives to private players. The net effect of the DPLA, plus common approaches to the physical storage of books and digital preservation, should be to free up local libraries to provide extremely valuable services directly to their communities. If the DPLA is successfully built and the public never knows about it but comes to love their local libraries even more, then the DPLA movement will have been an enormous success.

T HE DPLA IS not the only initiative in the world to create a national digital library. In fact, many countries are still ahead of the United States in this regard. The South Korean national digital library opened in 2009, with a physical headquarters in Seoul. The largest network of national digital libraries, Europeana, brings together cultural objects in digital format from many of the countries in Europe. Instead of building a single global digital library, these national initiatives can be linked together in a way that helps people find information across geographic boundaries.

Europeana provides anyone with access to over 23 million digitized cultural objects in Europe, including books, manuscripts, maps, paintings, films, museum objects, archival records, and other digitized materials. Thanks to funding from the European Commission, Europeana draws its content from a network of more than 1,500 cultural heritage institutions that provide metadata either directly or via aggregators in order to facilitate access to locally stored objects. Europeana's mission is to enable "people to explore the digital resources of Europe's museums, libraries, archives and audio-visual collections . . . [and to] promote discovery and networking opportunities in a multilingual space where users can engage, share in and be inspired by the rich diversity of Europe's cultural and scientific heritage."[11] Europeana also addresses some of the key obstacles facing the digital heritage industry, including the legal issues that arise about what constitutes the public domain when user engagement meets linked open data.

In partnership with Europeana, the DPLA community is focused on building a global network of national digital libraries. The DPLA staff find creative ways to highlight content from digital collections that make sense in an international context. Recently, the DPLA launched an exhibition in collaboration with Europeana to showcase resources from some of the DPLA's content providers. The exhibition, entitled "Leaving Europe: A New Life in America," enables web searchers to explore the motivations and journeys of European immigrants to the United States in the nineteenth and early twentieth centuries. The exhibition draws images and documents from across Europe and puts them alongside content from the National Archives and Records Administration, Harvard University, the New York Public Library, the University of Minnesota Immigration History Research Center, and other US institutions. By combining photographs and other documents from both sides of the Atlantic to create an exhibition, the DPLA and Europeana created an entirely new means to conceptualize immigration to the United States, while highlighting the sorts of original documents that users can access through their digital collections.[12]

As national digital libraries and regional initiatives such as Europeana come online, the job of librarians can be to help link them in ways that are useful for their patrons. The creation of shared exhibitions online is only the starting point. Librarians have an essential role to play in curating and presenting these exhibits, which make sense of the vast materials that digital libraries make available. Linking national digital collections leads to vast possibilities for new scholarship as well as fascinating ways for anyone to deepen their understanding of the history of civilization.

W E DO NOT know what form libraries and the web itself will take over the next ten to twenty years—whether they will move toward an increasingly commercial, locked-down, profit-oriented set of systems or toward a balanced ecosystem that includes compelling public options. The better future is one in which we value both economic incentives and the strong public interest in freedom of information and information privacy. People should be able to make money as authors, publishers, agents, booksellers, and search engines, but they should also be able to access information through libraries on a "free to all" basis. That balanced future is possible, but societies will need to be clear about their goals and assertive in their choices to bring it about.

Libraries will be able to thrive and innovate in a networked, digital, and mobile era only if they adopt the collaborative approach of building shared platforms. Libraries as platforms—ideally, free and open platforms—must be a core part of library infrastructure in the future. If libraries do not make this shift, the companies that have already figured it out—search engines, social networks, even doll companies— will play a bigger role than libraries in the shaping of democracy in our digital future.

Chapter Five

Hacking Libraries
How to Build the Future

Information is alienated experience.
—Jaron Lanier, *You Are Not a Gadget* (2011)

L IBRARIES HAVE SERVED as iconic institutions in societies for thousands of years. In their modern public form, they fill an essential role in democratic systems: to inform, engage, and delight people in communities by making knowledge freely accessible. In their modern academic form, they serve as laboratories for scholarship, learning, and co-creation at all levels of schooling and research. As archives and special collections, they serve as the repositories of knowledge for our societies as well as essential means to access the histories they contain. These jobs are crucial to the proper functioning of any open society.

In the digital world, libraries ought to continue to serve these essential functions, just as they have in the analog past. Libraries should never stop providing access to information and knowledge, embracing and making possible the best new scholarship, and preserving our stories and our research findings for posterity. We should keep expecting, and investing in, these services in the interests of promoting a wide range of public goods: civic engagement, teaching and learning in schools, happiness and entertainment, and other salutary ends. The need for public-spirited institutions to serve these essential functions is even greater in the digital era than in the analog era. The common argument that we need fewer libraries in the era of Google is faulty to its core.

Two important paradoxes of digital life make clear this growing, not diminishing, importance of libraries. The first paradox is that information that has been digitized may be easier to access than ever before, but is very hard to preserve. Digital information may even prove to be more expensive to preserve than its analog form, counterintuitive as that may sound. These dual functions, access and preservation, have long been well served by libraries. In a digital world, we have mobile devices, personal computers, and powerful search engines as means to access information from anywhere, at any time, at low cost. If the information that people want to access is freely available on the web, for instance, the job of providing access to it is relatively straightforward.

The challenge lies, however, in successfully preserving digital material. Although some information will live a long time (too long in fact—think of the embarrassing photograph on Facebook, the rumor about professional misconduct, the scathing blog post written in haste and anger), some of the information that we hope persists will not. This phenomenon—known as "data rot"—is an enormous challenge that will keep digitally savvy librarians employed for a long time. We will need smart people who can figure out how to save what we need to save and let the rest fade away.

The second paradox, and the subtler of the two, is that while information is ubiquitous in wealthy societies, it is often too hard to find, to make sense of, and to use. What's worse, digital information is not democratically distributed. It may look ubiquitous, as though anyone can access it, anytime, for free, but digital information remains far from evenly distributed. We still face a slew of digital divides, in that some people simply have better access to good computing equipment, fast network access, and digital literacy skills than others. These divides commonly fall along socioeconomic lines: those who are wealthier and better educated are more likely to enjoy the benefits of the digital era, and those who are less well off are more likely to be on the other side of the digital divides. Libraries are perfectly positioned to bridge these divides, both today and in an increasingly digital future.[1]

The way in which libraries fulfill these two classic functions—providing access to and preserving our cultural and scientific heritage—necessarily must change from the way it has been done in the past. The shift under way in libraries today is on the right track in many places, but too often the process of change is too slow and too poorly coordinated. The rate of change varies enormously from the most forward-looking institutions to the most traditional. If change continues in this desultory fashion, it will be impossible to make the most of the best innovations—and it may prove too late for most libraries, which may wither for lack of support.

The way to make positive changes for the public is for the library profession to continue doing what it has long done best—ensuring access to and preservation of information—and simultaneously borrow modes of operation from the culture of the web. This combination can be enormously powerful. Librarians have historically been leaders in making information broadly accessible, preserving culture over the long term, and meeting ancillary but important societal goals, like the protection of individual privacy and autonomy. These goals should continue to guide libraries into the rest of this century and beyond. In all kinds of libraries, modes of operation and specific functions are changing—and need to change more, and more quickly—but not these core goals. The way to bring this change about is to hack libraries.

THE SPIRIT OF hacking has much to offer librarians seeking to usher in a brilliant new era for libraries. "Hacking" has come to mean something in the public discourse that is remote from its origins. People commonly think of hacking as a destructive act and believe that hackers are either pimply teenagers in their pajamas writing computer programs to mess up other people's systems or Russian spies out to steal their identity. Hackers are commonly viewed as people who have no regard for intellectual property and believe that information is meant to be free, without any kind of restriction.

It is not these destructive hackers that we should turn to for inspiration, but the hackers in the classic sense—those who brought us the open and configurable computers, networks, and programs that we rely upon today. The hacker ethos, in its positive sense, dates back to the early days of the computing revolution in the 1950s and 1960s. The hackers who have something to teach us are those who wrestled with the original, massive computers of the 1950s, those who worked in the MIT artificial intelligence (AI) lab in the late 1960s and 1970s, and those who followed Richard Stallman in creating the Free Software Foundation.[2]

The hacker ethos in the positive sense is about the ability to deconstruct and reconstruct information systems. In the case of libraries, the task is to figure out how to break down the functions that libraries need to serve and then to rebuild those functions for the digital-plus era. Some patrons choose to read a book, for instance, in its basic, digital form, whereas others may choose to buy the print version because they prefer hard copy. The same is true of a newspaper or an image or just about anything else that libraries curate and provide to their users. Through hacking—breaking down functions and figuring out how to reconstruct them—libraries can meet these various needs.

The idea of hacking libraries might sound faddish—or worse, empty—at first blush. It is, in fact, a serious and fundamental proposition that is meant to draw us back to an approach based on the first principles of library work: finding the best ways to provide access to knowledge in the near term and preserve knowledge in the long term. This approach is grounded in a belief in the power of open and freely configurable systems and information. Today's library students get the premise, if their blogging is to be believed; those interested in paying attention as the story unfolds can follow the student blog Hack Library School.[3]

Hacking libraries is a mode of operation, not a specific task. The process of remaking libraries needs to be, first off, conceptual: we need a frame of reference for the reinvention of institutions that a broad community of theorists, practitioners, and funders can support. The idea of hacking libraries begins with engaging a large number of people from a diverse array of communities, joined by a common cause: to remake libraries as institutions and to train or retrain librarians to thrive in the years to come. Hacking libraries, in other words, will serve the public interest.[4]

Hacking libraries starts with reconceptualizing libraries. To hack libraries is to start by replacing the library as place with the library as platform, each library being a node in a series of interconnected platforms. The library will continue to house physical materials and provide a space for people to go to and interact with information; librarians will continue to be helpful guides through the world of information and knowledge, present in both the physical environment and online. But the core function of the library and those who work in them will be dramatically more networked and interconnected across institutions.[5]

Hacking libraries would alter the long-standing traditional library model, which involves obtaining physical copies of materials; bringing those physical materials—books, CDs, microfilm, and so on—to a central location; sorting materials in ways that help people make sense of and find them; and keeping those materials safe for the long term. Each of these functions, in a world of hacked libraries, would be shared among a network of libraries. Libraries would share much more extensively the work of choosing materials to keep locally; creating original catalog records, bibliographic materials, and useful commentary; and ensuring long-term preservation of the collected sets of materials in particular places or fields. Individual libraries would then be free to split activities between collaborations with others and direct assistance to their own library users in accessing these shared platforms.

Hacking libraries would also shift their emphasis from materials-centric to consumer-oriented. Instead of focusing on building collections, many librarians have come to see their primary job as serving people at various stages of their lives. A library that is oriented not toward materials but toward people will be more explicitly service-focused, meeting immediate and relevant needs rather than continuing to do only the work they traditionally have done.

A strategy of focusing on people rather than on materials is risky and would require libraries to stop doing some valuable things that they've done in the past, especially those activities related to building and managing redundant collections. In any given metropolitan area or consortium of colleges, such a strategy would entail holding and caring for fewer copies of physical materials, for instance, and relying more on digital, networked configurations and materials. But there is greater risk in failing to make this change in orientation.

A FEW OF THE great libraries of the world have begun hacking from another angle: their digitization initiatives are making major collections available to the public online. Digitization is a part of hacking libraries because it breaks down the idea that libraries have an exclusive claim on the materials they hold. The special collections of the New York Public Library, for instance, and some of the great libraries of European universities are being digitized, bit by bit, in a way that makes them freely and broadly available online, not just at the physical library but from any computer anywhere in the world. These digitization efforts are enormously valuable. They offer immediate access to materials that were previously available only to those able to get on airplanes and secure privileges to visit once-exclusive libraries, and they offer a supplementary means of preservation of physical materials that might become brittle, fade, or otherwise fall apart over time. These digitization initiatives at major libraries also teach us about the process of digitization and the sharing of materials online.

The value of these early initiatives to many different types of people is already becoming clear. Even when the process of digitization is uncoordinated, as it so often is today, the rates of usage of digitized materials prove the benefits of investing in making collections available on an open access basis. In a networked world where libraries function as platforms, digitization takes on greater value over time as more and more people and materials are added to the network.

Once digitized, materials from around the world become immediately useful to people who might not otherwise have known that they even existed. A global network of libraries and librarians, once coordinated, can alter what can be learned from anywhere. Within moments, and with a few clicks, a student working on a school physics project can find himself zooming in on the notebooks that Sir Isaac Newton used in 1661. One more click, and the same student can be listening to a BBC radio production that puts the notebooks in context. The thrill of the encounter with this original material, as well as the multimedia secondary sources, would have been unthinkable a decade ago. The student's sense of wonder is possible because the University of Cambridge decided to invest in curating, digitizing, and putting Sir Isaac Newton's personal materials online and making them freely available, and because Cambridge also partnered with the BBC to create the radio production that helps any listener make sense of Newton's scribbling. The digital text and the link to the BBC program were not randomly linked but were made proximate to one another by a helpful librarian.[6]

The benefits of making materials available online may seem obvious, but it could not be more revolutionary for libraries and archives. There was once a view that libraries should keep the most valuable materials under lock and key, away from those who had not been blessed with the privilege to access them. Fortunately, very few librarians subscribe to this theory of scarcity today, at least not in theory. In reality, however, many special collections still operate in the old-fashioned, proprietary way. Alluring original, historical materials are locked away in collections that may or may not be cataloged. There is no way for a scholarly researcher, much less a school child or her teacher, even to know that they exist, much less be able to find them. Often the librarians or archivists responsible for the materials don't even know everything that is in their care.

Especially as we digitize, we should not throw away the practice of preserving materials in print form. Original materials ought to be kept, in analog format, both for security and for preservation. The rarest objects are kept under the highest security. After all, we would not dream of putting an original copy of the Declaration of Independence in the equivalent of a library petting zoo where anyone interested in touching it could feel the corners of the paper. Special collections have been looted in the past by those who know the value of these holdings. Rare maps, for instance, can be sold on a black market. Edward Forbes Smiley III admitted in court in 2006 to having stolen ninety-seven rare maps from six major libraries, including Yale, Harvard, the New York Public Library, and the Boston Public Library. Smiley had the trust of librarians who gave him direct access to valuable maps, which he cut out of the books that held them using an X-Acto knife.[7]

Nevertheless, there is no reason why digital copies of original materials, set in helpful context, should not be widely and freely available. Many cultural heritage institutions, including libraries and museums, worry about sharing their most valuable treasures in digital format online. Even if the costs of digitization, digital storage, and preservation can be met, the keepers of many special collections worry that making their holdings available for free online will not serve their institutions well. The most-cited concern is that fewer people might come to see the physical materials if digital replicas can be accessed from home.

This fear about digital copies dissuading people from visiting libraries and other institutions turns out to be ill founded. Not only does foot traffic not go down for those libraries that digitize their treasures, but it often goes way up. The best of the digital presentations of library, archive, and museum materials have helped institutions bring more people through their doors. The Tate Modern, the Brooklyn Museum, and the Harvard libraries, for instance, have all invested substantially in the digitization of special collections. Libraries, archives, and museums routinely report that putting their digital collections online increases foot traffic because people are inspired to see the originals.

Other stewards of these materials fear piracy. They contend that the existence of digital copies on the library network will enable others somehow to profit from their special collections. This fear is roughly analogous to the concern of the music industry that digital files of sound recordings would lead to piracy. Although music companies have struggled mightily with the digital transition, the problem has not been the mere availability of digital files of the music; in fact, digital sound recordings have led to fast-growing sales of the music itself and many ancillary products through iTunes, Spotify, and many other services. Piracy has also been largely limited to popular new music that appeals to young people, while classical music and jazz, for instance, have not been adversely affected in the same manner. There is no clear reason why the effects of digitizing a new Adele or Jay-Z song should be analogous to the digitization of a scholarly notebook or the painting of a great master.

A related concern about digitizing library, archive, and museum materials is that doing so will cut off a business model that might be attractive in the future. Those who hesitate for this reason are wondering whether there might be a stream of revenue for cash-strapped institutions if they could license their most valuable works in some fashion. They fear that they will lose a way to create scarcity in the works over time if they are available online.

This "future business model" objection to digitization and the sharing of materials from our cultural heritage institutions misses the mark in several ways. First, very few institutions have materials that could ever be exploited in this fashion. The most famous of paintings, books, sound recordings, and moving images might be used to generate revenues for the Louvre or the most exclusive of special collections libraries. But most materials are not likely ever to rise to a level of value that would make them worth exploiting in this manner. Very often, this "business model" objection is raised by tiny institutions that have wonderful materials but no possible market for exploiting their value in any serious economic sense. Second, it is unclear that making a digital copy accessible, set in context for those who wish to learn from it, would preclude any specific future use, including the monetization of the original. The fact that a painting from, say, the Peabody Essex Museum in Salem, Massachusetts, is digitized and online does not prevent the museum from charging a licensing fee for someone to make use of that image on a book cover. Most important, cultural heritage institutions exist in the first place for the purpose of making these kinds of works *available*, not to make them *scarce*. The mission of these institutions should be to take advantage of what the digital era can make possible, not to hesitate in the interest of preserving a conceivable future way to make money.

The most important move in hacking libraries, archives, and museums is to launch a mass digitization movement. Materials of historical worth are more valuable the more broadly available they are, without people having to jump over high hurdles to learn about them, much less access them. We need to coordinate a massive effort to digitize our cultural heritage and make as much of it as we can freely available online, and libraries and archives should lead the way.

ANNEMARIE NAYLOR IS a library hacker. Frustrated by the idea of the English public sector "giving up" on the small rural library and by talk of cutting library budgets, she set about to create a new model for the community library. In 2013 she helped launch the novel Waiting Room in St. Botolph's, with help from the Essex libraries and a group of volunteers. Instead of trying to save the traditional library, Naylor and her colleagues decided to create a space where people could create and exchange knowledge in a public-spirited manner.

Once a bus station, the Waiting Room is now a creative space for Naylor's community—a colorful, attractive space with high ceilings and a flexible arrangement. Naylor calls it a "hack/maker/library space." People in the community are urged to propose events and activities centered on ideas, skills development, and creative enterprise. The space hosts workshops alongside the Micro Social History Museum, where local residents can share and preserve their photographs, memories, and stories of life in St. Botolph's. The space also functions as a café, bar, and event venue.

The Waiting Room has attracted a great deal of attention. Through the work of Naylor and others, the idea of this kind of community library has been taking hold in England and spreading from there. Sixty-five community discussions across the country demonstrated the public interest in new kinds of local libraries for a digital era. Naylor has also reached across the Atlantic and is partnering with librarians such as Nate Hill in Chattanooga, Tennessee, to improve her model and build a network. In concert with Hill and a third librarian, Marc De'ath, Naylor has established a new venture, "Common Libraries," to help communities determine their own information needs.

For Naylor and her collaborators, libraries are the answer to poverty, unemployment, and boredom. As a platform for the exchange of knowledge and information, Naylor's version of a library is deeply aligned with the specific needs and interests of her community, not based on a single view of what a library *should* be as a site for collections or as a public space. In some communities, the goal of the community library is to help teach skills to the unemployed and bring the uninitiated into the world of technology. In others, the focus falls on supporting entrepreneurship or aspects of the creative arts sector. There is no one-size-fits-all model for the community library.

What Naylor, Hill, and De'ath are doing across the Atlantic is a great example of how libraries can shift from competing with each other to collaborating. Had they not collaborated with one another, these three librarians would never have been able to launch "Common Libraries" and have the freedom and resources to rethink completely their local libraries. To some extent, the hack they have come up with has already been well under way for decades, but unevenly. Librarians are, by and large, some of the best collaborators in the world, and the library system has developed over many centuries into a powerful network. The human network of librarians already has many of the hallmarks of what it needs to become for a digital era. But more needs to be done if libraries are to survive an era in which resources are stretched further than ever before.[8]

Librarians have proven over and over that the profession is capable of extraordinary collaboration. More than forty years ago, a group of major libraries in Ohio recognized the importance of shared computing resources and established a partnership called the Online Computer Library Center (OCLC), which is now referred to primarily by its acronym. OCLC calls itself "the world's largest library collaborative." The library data and services provided by OCLC to 70,000 libraries around the world enables libraries to avoid a great deal of redundant work.[9]

The OCLC partnership has reduced the need for every library to create its own catalog record for every book or item it collects, creating enormous efficiencies. OCLC's WorldCat system, for instance, allows anyone with web access to search across the catalogs of a large number of libraries to locate books wherever they are in the country. WorldCat is simple, but it has proved that implementing even the simplest of systems can be remarkably useful to library patrons.[10]

There are many other great examples from the past of libraries collaborating, rather than competing, in order to serve people better. The interlibrary loan system, for instance, ensures that a library patron in Des Moines, Iowa, can borrow a book that is not physically available locally if it is available at a partner library in San Francisco, California. Librarians have established collaborative collecting networks in which each library agrees to take on primary responsibility for collecting and storing particular materials. The Boston-area law libraries have agreed to such an approach, for instance.

OCLC and other present-day collaborative endeavors are important elements of the library world, but they are not sufficient to drive the shift toward open, connected library systems. The existing collaborations do, however, indicate that librarians have a great deal of practice in working together well and that the interpersonal networks among libraries are already in place and will make the tricky next steps much easier to carry out.

Deep collaboration among libraries is on the rise, but it is still not the norm. Too few librarians and library schools participate in the kind of collaboration that will fundamentally reshape libraries for the digital era. The collaborations that can make a huge difference include the creation of shared open-source platforms, shared professional development opportunities, shared collection development, and coordinated mass digitization.

We need radical collaboration in libraries, far beyond what happens today—not collaboration at the margins or collaboration as afterthought. Librarians need to measure their success not as individual institutions, or people, but rather as collaborators working together to build a new ecosystem of information and meeting the needs of a rapidly changing group of users. This series of conceptual shifts will not come easily, nor will it be uncontroversial.[11]

The next phase of collaboration among libraries may prove to be harder. The development of digital libraries should be grounded in open platforms, with open APIs (application programming interfaces), open data, and open code at all levels. No one library will own the code, the platform, or the data that can be downloaded, "free to all." The spirit that is needed is the hacker spirit embodied by Code4Lib, a group of volunteers associated with libraries, archives, and museums who have dedicated themselves to sharing approaches, techniques, and code related to the remaking of libraries for the digital era.[12] At an international level, the community that comes together in conferences as part of the NEXT Library is up to the same task of hacking libraries through large-scale collaboration.[13]

Libraries will become more powerful the more connected they are to other types of learning institutions. Schools are an obvious point of connection. Libraries as platforms, with open APIs, could help American public schools, for instance, as they introduce the Common Core standards across the country. Openly accessible library materials that fit the Common Core could be made easily available to teachers and their students as they create new teaching plans. Open systems could also serve as sandboxes for students who are learning to code and to work with digital materials.[14]

IN A WORD association game, "innovation" and "libraries" do not often come together naturally. That is probably a bit unfair to the many librarians who bring to their work a spirit of experimentation and innovation similar to the spirit that created the Internet and the web. To promote further innovation in our libraries, however, we—the members of the public who rely on them—need to ensure that libraries and library hackers have the money, resources, and time they need to make this transition.

Librarians have an almost endless canvass on which to work today. In addition to all the books and images and other materials that already exist, librarians can also focus on managing and preserving the extraordinary amount of material produced anew all the time. As large corporate IT firms remind us in their advertisements, we live in an era of big data. Each day we produce 2.5 quintillion bytes of data. As a result, 90 percent of the data in the world were created in the last two years.

Librarians need to set out to help people make meaning out of the massive amounts of data that we produce. Most likely, the skills needed for providing this assistance will not be found in any single person. Libraries will have to develop teams of staff members who work together, in a mode of nearly pure experimentation, to meet these rapidly changing needs. The members of these teams will need computing and design skills that many librarians do not have today. And they will need an open infrastructure and a massive amount of open data and metadata with which to work.[15]

Librarians should work with all kinds of unexpected partners in this process of reinvention. Graphic designers and user experience experts can help librarians reimagine how digital shelves might present books and other materials in revealing new ways. Business consultants can experiment with new models for the e-lending of digital texts that will make better financial sense without violating the letter or spirit of the copyright law. Most important, librarians should be open to partnerships with those who love libraries and seek to serve the public interest at this crucial moment when reinvention is most badly needed.

The aim of hacking libraries is to infuse them with the spirit of innovation that will lead to successful and positive reinvention. Most of the innovation in how we create and use knowledge is occurring in the private, for-profit sector. Funded by ambitious venture capitalists and pursued relentlessly by entrepreneurial CEOs and their programming teams, the start-up scene has been cranking out successful new information-related projects for decades. Consider Google's search service, Amazon's Kindle, Apple's apps platform, and Facebook and Twitter as five possible entrants in the contest for most important information innovation of the past decade. Wikipedia, Mozilla, and Khan Academy might be contenders from the nonprofit side of the ledger. What is the biggest innovation to emerge from libraries in the digital age? That's very hard to answer, but in this time of change it's clear that the next big innovation in knowledge management should come out of the world of libraries. Libraries can offer important alternatives to the services provided by the corporate sector, which will always have incentives to offer biased, limited, and costly access to knowledge.

The good news for libraries is that there is still time to make this transition. Physical objects are not going away, for a few years at least, and the old ways of doing business in libraries still serve important day-to-day functions. But the window to make this transition is not going to remain open forever. Those of us who care about libraries need to figure out how to hack libraries and the larger systems in which they operate in order to remake them for the digital-plus era.

This call to hack libraries has nothing to do with destroying them and everything to do with rebuilding them in ways that will be useful, attractive, and sustainable as formats and user practices shift. Reimagining and remaking these beloved institutions will not be easy. Current library activities that have appeal for many people may have to fall by the wayside. The net effect of hacking libraries, however, will be to save them as institutions, to make them more helpful and better positioned to achieve their goals for the future, and to unleash creativity in ways that we can only speculate about today.

If libraries are to be hacked, the job of the librarian will have to change dramatically, and the curricula at library and information schools will have to be rewritten. Just as important, we will need to find ways to reward different kinds of leaders in librarianship.

Chapter Six

Networks

The Human Network of Librarians

Librarian: Shelved or renewed? Glamour girl Google and her friends Bing, Yahoo and Cha Cha dethroned the trusty silencer of the stacks, our public librarian. Now, the local library is online, shoes and shirts are no longer required and we can use our "outdoor voice" indoors if we are so inspired. Will the decibel diva's future be shelved?
Verdict: *Evolved. Although virtual media and the Internet search deleted the Dewey decimal system, people still enjoy reading books the old-fashioned way and appreciate research help. The new librarian is a digital archivist, savvy with searches, keywords and helpful websites.*

—Heather Dugan, "12 Jobs on the Brink: Will They Evolve or Go Extinct?"
Salary.com, 2012

T HE ENTRY FOR librarian as a "job on the brink" on the Salary.com website recently made the rounds on many library listservs. "Really?" responded one talented librarian on her email list. She was right to be annoyed. We, as members of a democratic society, badly undervalue librarians and the role that they play in our republic. The job of librarian should not be considered a "job on the brink" by anyone. But the fear in the ranks is palpable in some corners of librarianship. And the risk to the profession—stemming from budget cuts and from a lack of understanding of the growing value that librarians can bring in a digital era—feels all too real in many quarters.

If one agrees with Eli Neiburger that "libraries are screwed" if they remain overly invested in the codex (the traditional form of the book), then a parallel view of librarians is true. If they remain overly invested in a traditional view of their jobs, focused on maintaining collections of physical objects, they too will face a harsh future. If libraries fail to garner more support and continue to see federal and state funding fall, librarian jobs will go away. The threat of layoffs is well known to librarians in every sector—school libraries, public libraries, academic libraries, special libraries, and archives. Librarians need to reinvent themselves and their profession and align what they do with what their communities need from them.

A hearty, innovative band of librarians is staring down these problems and starting to address them. Consider Jessamyn West, a librarian in rural Vermont. If each small-town library in Vermont sees itself as disconnected from the others, the likelihood that they will each continue to garner community support is very low, and West is determined to head off that outcome. On the other side of the country, in technology-loving California, Sarah Houghton is the director of the San Rafael Public Library. The library users of San Rafael have a range of needs, as in any community, but Houghton is demonstrating a special ability to lean into the digital inclination of her patrons. In Virginia, school librarian Melissa Techman worries about the political climate and the cuts that libraries have suffered—and she's determined to do something about it, using the network as an organizing tool. At libraries large and small around the world, library innovators are well aware of the pace of change in the world of knowledge and the threats they face if they do not adjust accordingly.

As they recast their profession, these library innovators are taking a page from the other big area of information and knowledge management of our era: the development of the Internet and the web. The growth of massive information networks has come about because those who have been involved in building them have worked in a highly collaborative, distributed manner. As an ethos of open participation has come together with a belief in the power of continuous innovation, the outcome has been a whole that is far greater than the sum of its parts. The World Wide Web, email systems, countless open-source development projects, social media, Wikipedia, and political movements like the Stop SOPA campaigns (a networked effort in 2012 to convince the US Congress not to vote for the Stop Online Piracy Act), all owe their growth and success to a radically networked, relentlessly innovative group of people working together—without being part of a single, traditional firm. This approach to change in the library profession, drawing on the principles of the web, is inspired.

The type of librarians who are thriving most consistently in the digital era are those who have found a way to operate as a node in a network of libraries and librarians. They are agents of change, actively creating the future instead of constantly reacting to it—or worse, resisting it. Jessamyn West, the librarian in rural Vermont, is one such creative, networked librarian. West is connected to her peers both in libraries and in other information-related environments, including the world of technology. She is partway through a project to visit all 183 public libraries in Vermont, which she is also mapping online using a service called BatchGeo. By meeting with librarians and library users across Vermont, West is learning firsthand about the needs of her colleagues and their patrons. West also sees beyond the immediate context in which she is operating: she seeks to operate at scale and to bring the best ideas in the library world to her patrons and her many readers on social media.[1]

The view of oneself as operating in a network, not in an independent silo, is essential to success for librarians. Sarah Houghton, the San Rafael library director, is a champion at networked communications and leadership. Here's how she describes herself on her popular blog Librarian in Black: "I am a big technology nerd and I believe in the power of libraries to change lives. Combined, they make a fearsome cocktail. I have been called an iconoclast, a contrarian, a future-pusher, and a general pain in the ass. I take great pride in each." *Library Journal* named Houghton one of its "Movers and Shakers for 2009" as a trend-spotter.[2]

Sarah Houghton's library in San Rafael has recast itself for the digital era. Neither overly committed to the past nor oblivious to the physical, the San Rafael Public Library is aiming its programs squarely at the digital-plus present in which its patrons are living. The library blends electronic resources, attractive events for kids, and traditional library services tailored to the interests of the public of San Rafael. Houghton also takes her case on the road, which enables her to bring the best ideas she encounters back to San Rafael and also to share with other libraries what San Rafael is doing. As a prolific public speaker and writer, Houghton makes the case for networked librarianship through her blog, on Twitter, and at conferences for the digitally infused library.

The aptly named Melissa Techman, a teacher and librarian in Albemarle County, Virginia, is another dynamic woman who is blazing the trail for librarianship. Techman fears that there is far too little collaboration at the local level in libraries. She has set out to connect with others in both the library field and the information management field and has gotten involved in all kinds of projects. Techman watches webinars, joins Google hangouts, and works continuously to develop an online network. Recently, she became involved with the National Writing Project and NEXMAP, which aims to add circuitry to the traditional notebook in a project called "Hacking the Notebook." If successful, Techman's innovative work could spread beyond the world of libraries to other settings in which students learn—where they learn to write, for instance. Techman runs a Pinterest board for *Library Journal* called "Cheap and Cheerful Librarian Tips," which links her interest in DIY arts-and-crafts projects with her library work.

Techman also sees herself as a political actor. More librarians need to see themselves in this light and to be prepared, as Techman is, for the inevitable hard conversations about library budgets and services. She has built an email list of her local library supporters who are willing to write to politicians to press them to avoid cuts to library funding when the inevitable budget ax begins to swing. Librarians like Techman know that their activities need to be tightly aligned with the needs of their communities and that they need to be loud about making the case for this alignment. The very same information networks that support libraries in sharing knowledge can help support librarians as political actors.

West, Houghton, and Techman are the kinds of librarians who are expertly bringing together the technology, library, and political worlds. Big libraries are also seeing the value of this combination of skills. Both the British Library and the Royal Library of Denmark now have "Wikipedians-in-Residence," people who have become adept at contributing code and text to what has developed into the largest online encyclopedia. They understand how networks work online, how people find information, and how new knowledge is created in online communities. Library staffs themselves must develop these kinds of skills in order to meet the needs of current library customers. Networked, collaborative library work makes the most of the great public information systems that are under development today, but these systems will not be much use if we do not have skilled *people* who know how to make them work for particular audiences. In the process, these networked leaders can work together to make the case for libraries in the political arena when it comes time to argue about where scarce budget resources should go.

Highly networked librarians are those who have developed new skills and who remain open to new ideas, but these skills and openness have not been consistently taught or encouraged in the library world. With the rapid emergence of the digital environment and the quick shift in user expectations, librarians have been forced to learn new skills every year in order to serve their patrons effectively—even as they struggle to accomplish all the things they have done in the past. In many library systems, there are too few hours in the day to do the research necessary to find the means of training and retraining, much less to accomplish this training. Given that public libraries are under major budget pressure, the notion of adding more staff or more hours to allow existing staff to take time off to retrain may seem preposterous.

And yet, if larger numbers of librarians do not soon invest the time and money necessary for this training and retraining, libraries as institutions risk falling behind. The reason why websites like Salary.com list librarianship as a candidate for "jobs on the brink" is that libraries and their staffs risk becoming obsolete as the learning, research, and entertainment patterns of their patrons change with time. Most library systems have failed to support their staff in retraining quickly enough to keep up with these shifts.

Before long, every library system will need to have on staff at least some librarians who are well versed—as West, Houghton, and Techman are—in the development and deployment of the most promising digital technologies. Ideally, most library systems will have librarians who are involved in the creation of the new digital environment through which many of their patrons are meeting their information needs. Most libraries, whether in the United States or elsewhere in the world, have few, if any, staff members who are up to speed on the most current technologies. And too few libraries have committed to helping to build the open, networked library platforms of the future. There are vibrant, growing communities of librarians doing so, especially as part of the open-source development and open-content worlds, but the total number of participants in these edge communities of librarians, compared to the total number of people working in libraries, is disproportionately tiny. That's where the problem lies.

Many of the skills and experiences that have served librarians well for the past century are still relevant—they're just not the *only* relevant skills. The preexisting skills and experiences that are still important include the ability to help patrons find the information they need, to anticipate other resources they might like or benefit from, and to take the long view when it comes to preservation, among many other skills. But no one would dispute the fact that new skills are helpful, if not necessary, for librarians to thrive in a digitally mediated universe. At a minimum, new tools make finding, creating, and storing information simpler and more effective, and librarians ought to be masters of them—if not creators of these tools themselves.

The good part of this story of rapid change is that librarians can take advantage of exciting new possibilities for serving patrons. The new skills that will prove most important for librarians have to do with designing, creating, and re-using new technologies, sorting credible from less credible information in a complex online environment, and partnering with people from all walks of life to co-produce information and new knowledge in digital forms.

Despite the external threats bearing down on the profession, librarianship can thrive in a digital and networked era. First, however, it needs to evolve, at every stage of professional life and in all types of libraries, archives, and cultural heritage institutions, to meet the needs of library users today. The deans and faculty members of library schools and information schools are well aware of the need for change, and many leaders are hard at work preparing the newest members of the profession. Many library schools, for instance, have transformed themselves into interdisciplinary iSchools as part of an international movement that acknowledges the importance of the networked world. Forward-looking institutions need to make aggressive, strategic investments in the professional development of existing library staff. And the profession at large needs to welcome the involvement of those of us outside the field who care about the fate of libraries.[3]

To prepare for this transformation, librarians need to reorient themselves and their institutions for scale. By this I mean that librarians need to focus not on individual, physical libraries but on the larger networks—physical and digital—of which their libraries are a part. This reframing for scale is exactly why Jessamyn West's approach to her work in Vermont—operating at network scale rather than at the level of a single library—is so effective. In the past, librarians were concerned with the immediate and the physical, and their job was to select from among the possible materials a subset to bring to their particular location. Librarians then offered these books, sound recordings, images, and videos to their patrons; occasionally they would also ship objects—at great expense and with a time lag—to library users in other towns. Despite the fast-changing world of technology, librarians today can help their communities so much more effectively than in the past, by more ambitious forms of sharing.

Now library users have vastly different needs and expectations, and the materials themselves are often available not as physical objects but digitally. The librarian's job has shifted from one of investing in physical, location-specific materials to a mix of activities that depend on a larger network. Librarians today must co-produce the network, make useful what can be found through it, and help people as they live in a networked world. Most forward-looking librarians, including Sarah Houghton at the San Rafael Public Library, have already reoriented their institutions this way. But because information companies are still far more effective at providing information services to people digitally than libraries are, much of our access to information may soon be mediated not by unbiased librarians but by profit-driven businesses.

An emphasis on scale will require that libraries adjust the duties of their librarians on staff. It will also prompt different kinds of hires as new librarians join the ranks. The essential job requirement is changing from an ability to manage physical materials—still required, but to a lesser degree than in the past—to a high degree of facility with digital networks. The job of the cataloger, for instance, becomes much more about finding ways to harness the extraordinary force of linked data in open systems and even crowdsourcing among knowledgeable persons than about determining subject headings in a cloister. Libraries also need to develop more skills within their network in related fields like community organizing, event planning, and business development.

A focus on scale will enable librarians to fulfill their most important task: finding ways to solve major problems that we face as a society. The essential point here is about alignment: libraries need to align their work with the needs of their communities. That is why Melissa Techman's efforts to determine community priorities and maintain a politically oriented online listserv are so crucial. An emphasis on scale and on helping people deal with the challenges of a digital era will enable librarians to find areas of comparative advantage in the years to come.

Unlike for-profit companies, for instance, librarians can help patrons sort credible from less credible information. In a world in which anyone can be a pamphleteer and a publisher, providing this service is central to librarians' comparative advantage. The mode of search and discovery and the provision of recommendations should be an area of major research and development in libraries, not left to the commercial sector to exploit. The gnarly and growing problem of how to preserve digital information in a complex, networked environment—where every book might be a "living book," subject to change at any time—is an obvious area for continuous development within libraries. These investments are happening in small pockets of the library world, but not in an especially coordinated way. It is time for more libraries and librarians around the country and around the world to collaborate on a strategy to address these issues.

T HE SKILLS THAT librarians need to develop, in order to operate at scale, look a lot like the skills that Google, Amazon, Mozilla, Khan Academy, and Wikipedia staff members develop through their day-to-day work. Creating these newly curated sites involves simple forms of computer programming, such as scripting. It calls for a design sensibility, both in approaching a known problem and in presenting information in a compelling way. New forms of metadata—data about the data—must be developed to help people find the most relevant information; librarians are awfully good at this already, but often don't practice this skill on the open web. What libraries risk in failing to adapt the skills of librarians is obsolescence.

Co-producing curated materials and metadata serves more than simply professional development purposes. One of the essential functions of presenting information at scale over the network is creating enough data about the materials to enable search algorithms to guide users to the most relevant materials. For instance, Google's PageRank algorithm, though secret in its particulars, is widely known to call upon the page rank of web pages that link to any given web page, as well as the search history of an individual, in order to render useful results. As large amounts of library materials come online, a huge need is arising for high-quality metadata to ensure that search algorithms return the best results first and less relevant results later.

Certain search problems cannot be solved without a co-production approach. Consider the problem of adding fine-grained location information to the records of digital materials. If someone is looking for images that relate to Shanghai, for instance, the knowledge that a digitized photograph comes from China is not as useful as knowing that the photograph comes from the city of Shanghai—or better yet, a particular neighborhood within Shanghai. To know that the photograph comes from the twentieth century is not as useful as knowing that the photograph was taken in the year 1949. The task of creating these data about digitized images is often straightforward, but it is a task that needs to be organized and carried out in a systematic fashion.

The function of adding good metadata about geographic location and data to an image file in a format that a search engine can understand might be performed by any number of people. The training of professional librarians would equip them well for this task, but there are a limited number of professional librarians and there is an endless amount of material that needs to have metadata added to it. While some high-value materials ought to be handled by professional librarians, the vast majority of materials in a national or international database might be managed by less well trained people. These volunteers might include a part-time worker at a small-town historical society or a resident of the relevant town. By coordinating a process that would allow interested individuals to help with metadata creation and updating, rather than doing all the work themselves, professional librarians could add vastly more to the digital commons. This crowdsourced model could be improved by developing systems to search for related metadata, which librarians and their volunteer colleagues could then simply edit rather than create from scratch. Quantum leaps, both for librarianship as a profession and in the amount of materials made available to the public, could be made by figuring out how to scale activities rather than doing everything by hand. Taking a page from the Wikipedia model, people could be convened periodically to work together on metadata creation and improvement, much as Wikimania each year brings citizen editors together to improve online encyclopedia entries.

Any discussion of crowdsourcing inevitably leads to a discussion about quality. Assessment of the quality of work is an essential part of any training or retraining of librarians. Teachers in every kind of education setting need to be much better at determining whether the learning process is working. No matter what the circumstances, teaching and learning processes can be improved over time. A feedback loop needs to be a part of the plan to retrain the library profession for the future, with assessment geared toward evaluating the fitness of the curricular materials, the effectiveness of the network model to deploy the trainings, and the value of the materials created by the trainers and the trainees as part of the curriculum. For instance, if the metadata co-creation process isn't improving the quality of the search results, then the training and development process needs to be rewritten. Web-oriented companies are excellent at putting such feedback loops to productive use in ways that the library profession can emulate.

This approach to the training and retraining of librarians for a networked age is not without its problems. For starters, many public librarians are not born hackers. They will need a structured experience in order to learn how to approach the most fundamental activities, such as scripting and using an open API (application programming interface). Today they may not even be able to experiment with such technologies if their in-house computer systems are restricted by their IT departments. Moreover, early adopters of digital librarianship will need to stop doing for a bit and start teaching, applying a "train the trainers" model.

The difficulty of getting training and retraining processes going in libraries should not keep us from at least starting somewhere. The benefits for the future of the profession are far greater than the costs. There is no question that faster development of coding and digital curation skills will be helpful to many individual librarians throughout their careers, as well as to the profession at large.

THERE ARE EXTRAORDINARY librarians in every age. Many of today's librarians, such as Jessamyn West, Sarah Houghton, and Melissa Techman, have already made the transition and become visionary, digital-era professionals. These librarians are the ones celebrated in Marilyn Johnson's *This Book Is Overdue!* and the ones who have already created open-source communities such as Code4Lib, social reading communities such as LibraryThing and GoodReads, and clever online campaigns such as "Geek the Library." There are examples in every big library system and in every great library and information school. These leaders are already charting the way toward a new, vibrant era for the library profession in an age of networks. They should be supported, cheered on, and promoted as they innovate. Their colleagues, too, need to join them in this transformation.

Just as individuals are changing the way they do their work, the nature of institutions is changing in a digital age. Many successful organizations are highly networked and porous, and libraries as institutions will also reap the benefits when they take advantage of the power of networks. The most effective libraries will be the ones that attract these extraordinary new librarians and enable them to be their creative best. Like all networked organizations, these libraries will measure their success by the quality of the collaborations they establish and by how well they share materials with their patrons compared to their peer libraries. In much the same way that networked organizations share employees, technology systems, and professional development opportunities, networked libraries will find ways to co-produce materials with their patrons. Together, they will be able to establish feedback loops of the sort that private-sector managers customarily put in place to ensure continuous improvement.

The transition in the library profession is still in its earliest stages. There is much more to be learned and to build on in the decade to come, and to date the library profession has not been in a posture of leadership as the newest information networks have developed at scale. But librarians have a great deal to offer back to the network and to the system of democracy, and the new generation of library leaders is here. In addition to West, Houghton, and Techman, witness the leadership of big-city library directors such as Amy Ryan in Boston, Tony Marx in New York, Luis Herrera in San Francisco, and Brian Bannon in Chicago. Each of these libraries has undertaken innovative major projects that are changing the way they operate and redefining great librarianship. The outcomes of these experimental approaches will be good for librarianship as a profession, for libraries as institutions, and for the concept and practice of democracy in a digital age.

Chapter Seven

Preservation

Collaboration, Not Competition, to Preserve Culture

Never believe a politician or a bureaucrat who says there's no money for preservation.

—Attributed to Charles Payton, founder of the conservation group TideChaser

H ISTORIANS A CENTURY from now may be justifiably angry with the current generation of library directors and archivists for a lack of foresight. During this transition time from analog to digital materials, we have yet to get a firm grip on the job of preserving born-digital materials of value. Formats shift every few years, making the job of even rendering files difficult after a decade or so. Much information that is created today—some of it of great potential historical importance—is disappearing more quickly than it should.

The future of libraries matters for many reasons, but their role in keeping the culture's knowledge safe over the long term is surely near the top of the list. Libraries are uniquely situated to ensure access to the knowledge that the public needs in order to be informed and engaged in life in a democracy. But an equally important job for libraries is ensuring that we preserve our cultural and scientific heritage in recorded form over time. Their ability to fulfill that long-term function is in jeopardy today for a number of reasons, including the fact that libraries are sometimes leasing access to materials, not buying them, and the preservation challenges presented by changing digital file formats.

When a great scientist at a medical school retired a century ago, an archivist from his university most likely would have knocked on his door and asked him to donate his papers. Ordinarily the scientist, flattered to have been asked, would have readily agreed. He would have spent a few months during his last year in his lab or office pulling his files together into a set of boxes that eventually would be picked up by the archivist and brought back to the library to be sorted, cataloged, and stored for the long run. These papers would have included his correspondence with other scientists around the world, notes from experiments, drafts of important papers, and perhaps working documents he had shared with medical school colleagues. As a result of this orderly process, his papers could be easily accessed today—probably out of newer boxes—from the university's archives and pored over by those who care about the history of science.

Consider the parallel case today. A medical school professor set to retire in 2015 has just been approached to turn over her papers to the same university archive. The friendly archivists ask for the same types of materials—correspondence, lab notes, and the like—but today's scientist has a much harder task. How much of her email correspondence has she kept? What kind of correspondence does she have with fellow scientists anyway? After all, when she seeks the latest scientific results, she doesn't ask anyone to send her their findings—she knows where to find them on an open-access web portal and just downloads them directly to her laptop. For some time now she has been scrawling her lab notes into a tablet PC. Her draft papers have never been printed out. Did she back them up before the papers were published? She can't remember. She hadn't been thinking about long-term preservation as she hustled for grants, sweated through peer reviews, hopped on planes to present her findings at yet another conference. She remembers that she has a whole lot of PowerPoints—perhaps those would be of interest? But then again, many of them have links to papers and images that would probably be broken at this point. And what if she decides just to turn over a few of her computers to the library and call it a day? What will the friendly librarian do with them?

The challenge of preserving the work records of scientists and scholars is a trickier proposition than it was a hundred years ago. The puzzle of what to keep and what to discard is a perennial issue for archivists, but that problem is exacerbated by the variability of formats so common today. The interconnections between files—many of them no longer "attached" to the original file—make for immediate challenges. But as one drills deeper into the issue, the problem gets much harder, not simpler. The archivists have obtained the files, but now what? How should they store these varied digital files in order to ensure that they can be rendered successfully, with fidelity, by a researcher in the future?

The challenges associated with digital archiving have engaged many bright minds, including those at the National Archives and other major institutions. These archivists and librarians have not found a single easy, cheap, scalable solution to these problems, nor are they likely to. As each year passes, we are losing essential materials that we ought to be preserving for the historical record. If the institution in question is not a massive institution, the simplest approach right now is sometimes to print out what we can to be stored the old-fashioned way. But this shortcut—a hack in the negative sense—is not a long-term solution, as much of the fidelity of the original files is automatically lost. We have to invest in finding systematic ways to do better.

U NIQUE ARCHIVAL MATERIALS present the most visible long-term preservation problem, but the issue is just as complex when it comes to published materials. The job of preserving knowledge in the form of published materials— books, maps, images, sound recordings, videos, just about anything that might hold knowledge—is an intricate one that has only gotten harder over time. The preservation issue is complicated today by the growing amount of material published, the variety of publishing formats, and the shifting modes of materials acquisition.

As challenging as it is to carry out, long-term preservation needs to be more effectively coordinated than it is today. It also deserves more investment, particularly at this moment of transition between analog and physical materials. Most libraries today have given up on the idea that any one institution can hold a "complete" record. Whether this was ever the case, it surely is not the case today. Although redundancy of records is helpful, it is not essential to have as many libraries collecting the same things as their peers in physical format and paying to store these materials over time. The vast majority of physical holdings at libraries are rarely, if ever, consulted. This is why it is so important to develop a network of libraries and archives, rather than continue to rely on a set of stand-alone institutions. One benefit of a network is that libraries can share the workload; another is that they can learn more from the experiences of others. Fundamentally, this type of collaboration will ensure that materials do not fall through the cracks as the volume of information and the diversity of formats grow with time.

Libraries are building on past efforts to form consortia to ensure that the record is preserved over time. These consortium-based approaches allow participating libraries to de-accession—to take out of their collections some physical materials that they know are held reliably at partner institutions. This collaborative approach is essential to the sustainability of libraries. The space, time, and money involved can be put to more effective uses elsewhere in libraries and archives.

Library and archival consortia preserve the cultural and scientific record in some fields and some geographic areas very effectively, but overall they form an incomplete patchwork. In some fields of knowledge, librarians and archivists have built explicit consortial relationships to ensure that certain records, such as court judgments, are maintained over time, but otherwise the system of preservation of knowledge is incomplete, and getting more so every year as more is published and in more formats. Certain valuable materials will be lost forever in the gaps of this patchwork system. There are great consortia to support, and they are growing, but it is necessary to continue to support and to build them as the digital revolution rages on.

Publishers, too, have a role to play in the preservation of the record, but they cannot serve as the archive of last resort for the works they publish. As a new library director, I was fascinated when a publishing representative came to visit me to ask for access to materials that his company had once published. The publishing house needed access to copies of books that it had published long in the past. It turns out that as many of the great publishing houses of the past have been bought by conglomerates and made into more efficient firms, some of them have not kept copies of all of the books they published. Libraries often hold the only copies, and publishers need print copies of their books in order to digitize them for resale as files in databases. Along the same lines, when Google wanted to amass a digital library of books, it didn't go to the publishers. Google approached several of the big universities in the United States and Europe to digitize their collections, which, taken together, approached completeness of record. Although publishers can certainly be counted on to have copies of materials their firm produces for some period of years, societies need a backstop in the form of libraries and archives.

Federal and state agencies are another possible candidate for this long-term preservation role when it comes to published materials. In the United States, the Library of Congress and the National Archives play major preservation roles, but neither institution can reasonably claim to hold a complete record of our cultural and scientific legacy—especially in an era when much of the publishing takes place on the web. State depository libraries preserve aspects of the record, such as the published law of a given jurisdiction. Overall, the state and federal systems work fairly well—though imperfectly— for printed and mass-produced materials, but they break down quickly as new formats are introduced and the scale becomes even greater and spikier. Twitter, for instance, reports that more than 500 million tweets are sent per day; on a busy day, spikes can lead to more than 25 times that many tweets, reaching a rate of as many as 143,199 tweets per second (on August 2, 2013).[1]

University libraries and large city libraries such as the New York Public Library also play important roles in the preservation effort. These large institutions preserve vast collections, chosen with enormous care over the generations by skilled bibliographers. The overlap between these collections is remarkably low, however, as Google found when it began its mass digitization of books. If well coordinated, a little overlap can be a good thing; if poorly coordinated, it is downright worrisome.[2]

The way forward on preservation is through large-scale collaborations at multiple levels, ranging from the international and national to the state and local. University libraries and enormous city libraries have established promising collaborations. The HathiTrust stands out among these collaborations as the most important. By joining together sixty major institutions, the HathiTrust is designed to ensure that the cultural record is both "preserved and accessible long into the future." HathiTrust, based at the University of Michigan, has preserved over 10 million volumes. They are not all accessible at any given time to all people who would like to use them, but they are held in trust for posterity. The HathiTrust could well evolve to make an extraordinary amount of digital material available to an extraordinary number of people.[3]

The Digital Preservation Network (DPN) offers a related promise at a national level when it comes to long-term preservation techniques and processes. DPN, led by the University of Virginia's James Hilton and his partners, brings together large university libraries to "ensure that the complete scholarly record is preserved for future generations." DPN's network model makes a great deal of sense. Rather than each university investing in its own preservation technology systems, repositories for knowledge, and redundant copies of many materials, DPN offers the promise of coordinated activity that leads to substantial innovation and more freed-up time and money for participating libraries. Through coordinated action, the record of knowledge can also be more reliably preserved. While DPN is at an earlier stage than HathiTrust, it offers a complementary vision. An important piece of the preservation puzzle is coming to consistent agreement on standards and methods of digital preservation. Though missing today, this puzzle piece might turn up through a collaborative effort like DPN.[4]

Collaborations that emphasize preservation on a field-by-field basis are also important. In the case of legal materials, the long-term preservation issue might seem simple: the people who publish the laws, whether federal, state, or local, ought to ensure their preservation. But it isn't that simple. The court system, for instance, is constantly strapped for funds. There is no consistent means for publishing and preserving legal materials at every level in the United States.

Although the Library of Congress contains a wonderful law library and major universities have rich law school collections, there is no comprehensive map that shows where legal materials are preserved for the long run. One problem is deciding who exactly is going to do the preservation—and determining whether that party is doing it properly. Another big problem that collaborators need to address is how to locate and provide access to materials in archives, large and small, across the country. Once located, librarians can focus on providing the context and service that they are so good at.

Law librarians have set in motion a series of innovative collaborations that could meet the challenge of preserving legal materials over the long term. The Law Libraries Microform Consortium (LLMC) has an old-fashioned name but an enduring goal that fits the digital era neatly: "preserving legal titles and government documents." The LLMC and the related Legal Information Preservation Alliance (LIPA) ensure that legal materials are stored in multiple places and multiple formats, including shrink-wrapped hard copies placed in underground salt mines in the middle of the country. Digital materials and those print materials held locally can be easily provided to people who need access, while another copy is held in a "dark archive" in case of catastrophe. As Nicholson Baker argues convincingly in *Double Fold*—a seminal book about the importance of long-term preservation of materials—it makes sense for us to keep a copy of original documents somewhere if we can manage it.[5] But it is not necessary for all libraries to hold all the same things, and collaborations like these keep them safe in the knowledge that they can turn to a peer institution to get materials to their patrons.[6]

Large-scale digital collaborations, such as the Digital Public Library of America, could also help local libraries focus their attention on more profitable matters. As leading public librarian and blogger Nate Hill wrote to a listserv about the possibility of the DPLA focusing on the Federal Depository Library Program (FDLP), a particular set of content for shared storage: "This seems like an opportunity for the

DPLA to scale up the solution to a problem I'm facing locally in Chattanooga. I have an enormous stash of FDLP docs that are almost never if not never accessed. To get rid of them is a next-to-impossible nightmare. At the same time, retaining these documents for public access has very little to do with my core mission and service delivery priorities here. I want them out of this building." The long-term preservation of materials need not be a burden to overstretched and understaffed public libraries in locations where large-scale, collaborative projects can easily bear the load more efficiently. There are much better uses to which a star librarian like Nate Hill can put his time.[7]

The same type of library collaboration is coming together at the state and local levels. In the state of Maine, for instance, academic and public libraries have teamed up. Faced with budget cuts and growing pressure to do new things, eight major Maine libraries are coordinating how they manage their print collections. The project enables these eight libraries to compare their collections and determine what to purchase and what to retain as a consortium, not as stand-alone institutions. This type of collaboration is booming—and for great reasons. No library can afford to go it alone anymore when it comes to print or digital collections, especially at a moment when both are needed.[8]

Binary agreements joining two major institutions can also play a positive role in long-term preservation and free up resources for libraries. In New York, visionary library directors Jim Neal at Columbia University and Anne Kenney at

Cornell University have signed an agreement called "2CUL" (pronounced: "too cool") to find ways to share resources in substantial ways. Backed with a grant from the Mellon Foundation, Columbia and Cornell are looking to share collections, services, and projects in a way that will benefit both communities. Their model is one that others should follow. Harvard and MIT, for instance, neighbors in Cambridge, Massachusetts, are collaborating extensively with one another, both in terms of libraries and in online teaching and learning activities. Instead of competing, library systems should put a priority on establishing the most effective partnerships they can.

As the costs of running a library rise and available funding falls, libraries are pressed to do more with less. Libraries have no choice but to de-accession materials with care, even as they add other materials to their collections. The long-term problem of preservation can only be solved by partnerships at multiple levels, since budget pressures and local needs vary between different kinds of libraries. In the academic environment, the fast-rising costs of journal subscriptions make many serials unaffordable. In public libraries, nearly every acquisition needs to be chosen with care. By coordinating more effectively, libraries of virtually every type can offer more materials to their patrons and increase the likelihood that these materials will be available for future generations.[9]

THE PROBLEM WITH materials preservation is neither a lack of concern nor a lack of effort on the part of librarians. The issue is well documented and has caused much worry, from the response to Nicholson Baker's *Double Fold* to a long series of research reports produced by librarians and archivists. Libraries and archives are starting to grapple with the newest and hardest of the problems, such as email and web preservation (which web pages should be formally archived, and at what intervals?), but the scale is vast and progress is slow. Extremely talented computer scientists have looked in detail at the problem of digital preservation and declared it very hard to solve. This issue cannot be tackled effectively without a team effort—and a lot more resources.

The risk is great that the transition to digital materials will result in societies losing more than they gain over the long run. One requirement of long-term preservation is certain: libraries and archives will need to collaborate with one another, at great scale, in order to get the job done over time. It is senseless for any single library to perceive itself as "competing" with peers on the sheer size of its collection. That viewpoint is a mistake. There can be no such competitive advantage in the long run, especially with the move to cloud storage and access for most materials; there is only the cost and distraction of housing physical materials that will never be consulted and are available in other formats at other libraries. Libraries need to collaborate so that they can free up other resources to meet the direct needs of patrons. Libraries can and should compete, in a friendly way, on the quality of the services they provide to their community members as they collaborate on the long-term job of preservation.

To put things in perspective, recall that all the great libraries of antiquity—including the libraries of Alexandria and Pergamum—have disappeared *completely*. However, the world did not lose the knowledge they contained when they disappeared. Some of what was held in those libraries had been moved to other locations, either to be copied or because it was stolen. Even the fate of the libraries of antiquity shows us that preservation relies not on the persistence of specific institutions, but on the proper functioning of a system that includes redundancy and the sharing of knowledge across institutions. There is a great deal more progress to be made in this respect during this transition to the digital age, but the importance of doing so is unmistakable.

Chapter Eight

Education

Libraries and Connected Learners

The time was when a library was very much like a museum, and a librarian was a mouser in musty books. . . . The time is when a library is a school, and the librarian is the highest sense a teacher.
—Melvil Dewey, 1876

THERE ARE 120,000 libraries in the United States alone. Libraries come in many different types and sizes, both in this country and around the world. When one thinks of a library in America, one might think of a familiar Carnegie library, set on the main street of a village facing a town green. Perhaps one thinks of the bustling branch of a major city library, tucked into a neighborhood. These libraries deserve their central place in our collective mind-set. At the same time, there are many other types of libraries that serve our democracy: academic libraries, special libraries, archives, and school libraries. School libraries are the most common type of library in the United States.[1]

The future should be bright for each of these types of libraries. Each serves a distinct and valuable function for the benefit of society, and each is worthy of support as it evolves. The school library, for instance, serves an essential function in supporting the work of public and independent school teachers as they prepare our kids for advanced study in college and for the workforce. Libraries of all kinds serve as partners to teachers, but there is a special and enduring role for school libraries and librarians. School libraries support all children as they learn to make sense of today's new information landscape, not just those who can afford to download any book they like onto their Amazon Kindle. Digital savvy should not be limited to those who can pay for it, and school libraries play an essential equalizing role in this respect. Yet school libraries are under great threat as budgets continue to tighten.

School libraries have faced a particularly hard time in recent years. Budget cuts eliminated federal support for school librarians in recent years. The Obama administration, strong on support for education as a general rule and long on rhetoric about the importance of libraries, has failed when it comes to championing school libraries. Instead, the administration has proposed cuts to federal funding for school libraries, which rely heavily on the federal purse for support. For instance, the president's 2013 budget proposal cut $28.6 million earmarked for literacy programs under the Fund for Improvement of Education.[2]

The vast majority of the libraries in the United States today—nearly 100,000 of them—are school libraries. That's a good thing, from an educational perspective. Data suggest a direct correlation between schools with strong libraries and academic performance. Studies show that students in programs with more school librarians and extended library hours score higher on English tests and higher on reading tests compared to students in schools where libraries have fewer resources.[3]

As we have seen, research data show that young people are more likely to use libraries than older people, in part because students are driven in their library habits by school assignments. A 2011 study by Pew Internet and American Life showed this connection: 81 percent of young people ages sixteen to twenty-nine said that they had read a book or other material for a school assignment, and many of them had turned to a library for access to that material. The same percentage of young people—81 percent—said that they had read a book for research purposes.

School libraries offer young people more than just access to the books and digital materials they need to complete assignments. The world of information is more distributed and complicated than ever before, and students need to learn digital literacy skills to be able to sort credible from less credible information. There are far more sources of information for students to choose from today than there have been in the past, but students are rarely taught how to make wise decisions about information quality.[4]

Librarians are naturals when it comes to teaching young people to understand information quality. Many schoolteachers who were trained in an earlier era struggle themselves with navigating the digital world of information and may not know how to teach kids well. This task of determining information quality is core to the library profession, and has been for decades, if not centuries. Though a struggle for many teachers, this educational challenge is one that school librarians are exceptionally well prepared to meet. It is the wrong moment to be cutting school librarians out of schools.

T HE PRESSURE ON school libraries is coming at just the wrong time. With school reform and major developments in education under way around the world, opportunities abound for strong, forward-looking school libraries to become even more important partners in meeting the needs of our schoolchildren. For instance, school libraries have a growing role to play in helping American schools and their students meet the new "Common Core" standards and their state-specific variants. School libraries can be great partners by coming up with the materials to support student learning. School librarians can also serve as vitally important teachers to meet aspects of the requirements themselves. For instance, the English and language arts Common Core standards specify that, "just as media and technology are integrated in school and life in the twenty-first century, skills related to media use (both critical analysis and production of media) are integrated throughout the standards."[5]

Adoption of the Common Core standards, approved by most states as of 2014, will gear much public school teaching and learning toward a shared set of particular themes and skills in mathematics as well as in English and language arts.[6] States can add specific materials to supplement the Common Core to meet local needs and educational goals. This book is not the place to debate the merits and demerits of the Common Core standards, but their introduction offers a useful jumping-off point for considering the role of libraries as schools change the way we teach students, whether in the United States or elsewhere.[7]

Schools need to adapt the materials that they use as texts to enable students to meet the Common Core standards and the state-based adaptations. Teachers need new ways to assess student performance, including new testing mechanisms and modes of feedback. Publishers are rushing to meet this demand for new teaching materials. Not all schools, however, can afford to pay the prices that Pearson, Houghton Mifflin Harcourt, and other school publishers charge for these new materials, and teachers are not universally well prepared to serve students in the new ways called for in the Common Core standards.

Teachers are rarely well trained in coming up with new materials or teaching new media and technology. Some are extremely savvy technology users, but most teachers were students before digital technologies became as central to the learning process as they are today. School librarians are trained in exactly these processes, both in graduate school as they earn master's degrees in library and information sciences and on the job in internships or first jobs out of school. A few leading institutions have taken up this challenge. For instance, the New York City Department of Education's Office of Library Services created a partnership with the City University of New York to develop what they call a "community of practice" around successful adoption of the Common Core.

For now, however, school librarians are fretting that they do not have the budgets to come up with the new materials required to do their jobs in partnership with teachers to meet the requirements of the Common Core. School librarians were also left out of the development of the standards; they should, however, be involved in their implementation. School librarians have terrific ideas about how to complement the teaching of the Common Core, ranging from presentation of digital and printed materials to new ways to engage students in talking about what they are learning.[8]

Matthew Winner, school librarian at Duckett's Lane Elementary School in Maryland, and his colleagues are examples of librarians who are leading the way in this respect. Sometimes Winner's teaching methods support kids' mastery of subject matter they explicitly need to know for the Common Core; other times he elicits interest in completely unrelated material.

The Common Core standards in mathematics for third-graders, for instance, call for these kids to "focus on four critical areas: (1) developing understanding of multiplication and division and strategies for multiplication and division within

100; (2) developing understanding of fractions, especially unit fractions (fractions with numerator 1); (3) developing understanding of the structure of rectangular arrays and of area; and (4) describing and analyzing two-dimensional shapes."[9] Winner's approach to teaching these core concepts involves a simple combination of a popular video game console, the Nintendo Wii, and newly digitized mathematics teaching materials. Instead of filling out mimeographed worksheets, kids earn points as they learn the math that is required for the Common Core. Kids certainly don't need to use video games to meet the new requirements, but this is one way in which school librarians can help develop and access digital materials and new teaching techniques to support classroom teachers as they make the transition to the Common Core.

Not all of Matthew Winner's work is directed toward teaching students things they need to know to meet the new standards, but the curricular materials developed separately by school librarians like Winner can be fully complementary to classroom teachers' materials, adding a crucial supplement to exercises that may be geared toward mastering the material bound to be on tests. Winner, unlike classroom teachers, has more freedom to develop supplemental lessons that aren't just about the bare bones, for instance, of fractions with a numerator of 1 but that introduce students to the wider world of information along the way. In another school setting, Winner has established "Earth Pals," a project-based experience for students in which they identify a local environmental problem to address. He generates spreadsheets of data for students to analyze, and in doing so, they learn not just about the software or about the environment, but also about how to process data in the context of problem-solving.

A parallel course at a school in Indiana, taught by Sherry Gick of Rossville Consolidated Schools, has taken up similar problem-solving themes. Students in the two classes use Skype to compare notes on their progress. Winner, Gick, and their network of friends share their findings publicly on blogs (The Library Fanatic, The Busy Librarian, and Andy Plemmons's blog at Barrow Media Center) and a wiki. Their students may do very well on the tests of related material included in the Common Core; their students may also have learned a series of related skills and had fun in the process, with librarians as their guides and teachers. A global teaching organization, the International Society for Technology in Education, saw the promise in this approach, granting the collaborators a prestigious Technology Innovation Award.

The development of national digital libraries might help here too. The Digital Public Library of America is designed to be a major source of support for school libraries as they seek to provide access to the digital resources children need to meet the new requirements of the Common Core standards. For instance, the Common Core standards call for the proportions of types of reading for young people to shift from 50 percent nonfiction and 50 percent fiction in the fourth grade to 70 percent nonfiction and 30 percent fiction by the end of high school. This shift toward "challenging informational texts in a range of subjects" can be supported by shared resources, collected at a national level and then curated locally to meet the needs of specific communities. The DPLA can provide access to school librarians and teachers to materials that meet the national standards, as well as provide a platform for uploading and sharing materials that are locally relevant. The Skokie, Illinois, school librarians might find useful the local examples shared by the Springfield, Illinois, school librarians, for instance, and vice versa.

Librarians such as Toby Greenwalt, now at Carnegie Library of Pittsburgh (and formerly of Skokie Public Library in Illinois, as it turns out), have been among those designing the new digital library systems and bringing new teaching materials online. Greenwalt comes at his work as a bridge-builder, someone who can translate the digital world for those who could use some help, including schoolchildren. Greenwalt has built library labs in public places, including schools, that allow kids to experiment with different modes of learning. Greenwalt takes the library concept and connects it to other learning environments. His outreach is bi-directional: in addition to bringing the library to schools, he even figured out how to tie a library card registration to school registration to encourage kids to use the public library. Greenwalt, one of the people helping to design the DPLA, is exactly the sort of librarian who is bringing school and library communities together through digital information and experimentation.

Just as important as the library's role in teaching digital literacy and helping students master the topics included in the Common Core is its place in schools and neighborhoods as an extremely valuable zone of learning outside of the formal classroom environment. In the United States, we provide too few opportunities for young people to pursue their passions if they don't happen to fit in prescribed curricular boxes. Libraries are zones where young people can be supported in creative pursuits that have little or nothing to do with mastery of the skills, such as the order of operations in math or how to succeed at reading comprehension, that are demanded of them in annual standardized tests. While these core skills are no doubt important, so too are the informal types of learning that draw young people into expansive, creative postures. Librarians can be extremely helpful guides in these informal and semiformal environments.

Matthew Winner, the Maryland school librarian and blogger, draws inspiration from working closely with students as ideas take on lives of their own. He strives through his work to put kids "center stage" and to give them the chance to figure out what they love and how to pursue it. Winner's concept echoes one of the central beliefs from our early republic. As Thomas Jefferson wrote to Isaac McPherson in 1813, "He who receives an idea from me, receives instruction himself without lessening mine; as he who lights his taper at mine, receives light without darkening me. That ideas should freely spread from one to another over the globe, for the moral and mutual instruction of man, and improvement of his condition, seems to have been peculiarly and benevolently designed by nature."[10]

LIBRARIES HAVE AN important role to play, too, as transformation takes place at the most advanced end of high school teaching. Since 1955, students who plan to attend college have been offered the chance to take Advanced Placement (AP) courses and the corresponding exams, administered by the College Board. These exams allow students to demonstrate their readiness to tackle the complex material ordinarily offered at competitive colleges.

Today AP exams are being rewritten, one by one. Certain exams have irritated some teachers by forcing instruction to focus on too broad a range of material in certain fields, such as biology and history. For instance, the AP history exam has been changed to emphasize early and recent United States history. This shift requires a change in the materials that teachers emphasize. Much of the useful teaching material is available in the holdings of university libraries and at government agencies, such as the National Archives. These big institutions are working hard to digitize and curate them for the use of teachers, and libraries are uniquely situated to facilitate this process.[11]

As the newly digitized material is built into school curricula, a national library-based initiative to make appropriate supporting material available to all AP teachers and AP students could drive down the costs of the transition to schools and enable students to have easy, free access to relevant study materials. School librarians can also help to prepare students for success in ways that complement the work of classroom teachers. It is one thing to put materials online, amid the trillions of bits of information accessible on the Internet; it is quite another to ensure that teachers have the right engaging materials at just the right time to help a student learn what she needs to master before taking the AP exam.

Once AP courses and the rest of high school are behind them and students cross the threshold into college, their research needs increase. At major research universities, students often encounter extraordinary new library resources. By contrast, community colleges serve nearly as many students as four-year, full-time colleges and universities, but without the strong library systems that their wealthier peer institutions can offer. In the United States, 13 million people attended community college in 2009—roughly the same number as attended four-year colleges. In contrast to the students for whom the AP courses might traditionally appeal, community colleges serve all Americans who apply, providing both academic and job training programs.[12]

Community college libraries tend to have vastly fewer resources than their better-funded cousins at four-year colleges and universities. Given their limited budgets, community colleges lack the ability to build a collection over time. Staffing levels are likewise nowhere near as high as at other academic libraries, forcing librarians to work overtime to meet the needs of students. And yet community colleges and their librarians have a major opportunity to serve vast numbers of students as learners, to increase job readiness for the highly skilled information-sector jobs, and to grow the economy in the process.[13]

A collaborative approach to building digital collections could serve students and faculty in community colleges especially well. A common technology infrastructure and shared materials, at either the international or national level, would enable community colleges to focus their limited library funds on hiring skilled librarians and providing them with ongoing professional development. Community college librarians would function much like the guides in other school libraries—helping students take advantage of the shared resources of the great libraries of the world rather than just the limited, local resources of the underfunded community college library.

EDUCATION HAS NOT yet been disrupted in the way that related fields—such as libraries and journalism—have been, but the crisis is coming. Especially in the United States, education has been plagued by a series of problems that we cannot ignore. Our system of teaching and learning is extremely expensive and not as effective as it should be. The United States does poorly compared to many other countries in K-12 education, according to nearly any metric or study cited. In some places, the problem is a lack of financial resources, but in many cases the problems facing education have little to do with money and much to do with management, outlook, and commitment.[14]

At the same time, information technologies are making it possible to experiment with new models of teaching and learning. In the higher education system, many leading universities have signed up with an entrant in the Massive Online Open Courses (MOOCs) horse race. Stanford and Silicon Valley's venture capitalists have spun out Coursera and Udacity, which have attracted many big-name collaborators. On the East Coast, Harvard and MIT have teamed up on EdX, which has drawn in heavyweight partners like the University of California at Berkeley and Wellesley College. These online platforms enable anyone, from anywhere, to take a free course on everything from artificial intelligence to intellectual property law. There are entrants in the race for the high school market too—Virtual High School, Florida Virtual Academy, Global Online Academy, the Online School for Girls, and many others.

Technology has made it possible to improve the quality of teaching and learning in both traditional and nontraditional ways. The most important recent innovation is Sal Khan's Khan Academy, a nonprofit that produces extremely popular, short videos and exercises that enable students to learn topics free, online, and at their own pace. A fifth-grade girl can teach herself computer science using simple online tools, for instance, in bite-sized chunks over several months or by gorging on multiple exercises over a single weekend. Students taking a high-powered math class might be struggling with a concept in their coursework and can turn to Mr. Khan's short, clear, effective videos to explain that same concept in, say, linear algebra in a way that provides the necessary "aha" moment for the learner. Mr. Khan's website has served more than 250 million learners, who use a combination of videos and exercises to master a broad range of material. Few teachers, if any, can claim to have touched so many people in such a short career.

The biggest disruption yet may come from a combination of for-profit publishing initiatives and computing. Consider the Amplify tablet, rolled out by the start-up education division of Rupert Murdoch's NewsCorp in the spring of 2013. The former chancellor of the New York City schools, Joel Klein, led a multi-year development effort to create a tablet for schools to teach the materials required by the Common Core standards. This tablet is beautiful, capable of incorporating open-source materials found elsewhere, and designed by teachers to teach skills and materials in a way that may prove highly compelling to students. Nevertheless, just as we probably don't want our kids to learn about history *only* through programs developed by the American Girl Doll company, we probably don't want any one publishing company to have too much control over educational materials and learning processes. There's a whole lot to be said for the free and unbiased information and access that libraries provide.[15]

Even if the American public school system does not decide to buy its teaching materials from Klein and Murdoch at NewsCorp, the shift to mobile and digital learning devices is on. This change is certain to disrupt the in-class teaching model on which schools have relied for centuries. Teachers in a recent survey surprised researchers by saying that they are requiring or encouraging the use of mobile devices in large numbers: 73 percent reported that they have asked students to use mobile devices and 45 percent reported using tablets in classes. These percentages of teachers encouraging the use of mobile devices represent a stark change from the recent past, when school districts had tended toward complete bans of similar technologies in schools.[16]

This trend in current practices toward allowing limited forms of inclusion of mobile devices in ways that are designed to improve the teaching and learning environment is likely to continue: as investment in better use of technologies in teaching leads to positive results, more and more schools will adopt successful practices. The large-scale shift toward blended learning models—where the best of old-school, analog teaching practices are combined with the best of the digitally mediated methods—is under way in schools and classrooms led by forward-thinking educators.

The effects of education reform could have a powerful—and positive—ripple effect into libraries. Libraries have a major role to play in this shifted teaching and learning environment. Librarians can support schools as they make the transition by providing access to the best, most relevant digital content. They can also serve effectively as teachers themselves, as well as mentors and connectors. The most sophisticated young people are learning in a more varied, complex, and interactive way than ever before and creating their own blended learning models as they find ways to learn and experience new things in new ways. Librarians can support these learners both in formal, school settings and outside of the classroom. The librarian's role is even more important for those who are less sophisticated in their use of digital media and need support in coming up the curve.

We need libraries to make a successful transition to the digital era for many reasons, but chief among them is their connection to other core democratic institutions. Especially at a moment of dramatic changes in teaching and learning, librarians need to work alongside educators to support students in informal learning and push them to think about the world beyond the classroom, about addressing local issues and problems, instead of focusing strictly on grammar or fractions. In the words of newspaper publisher Jack Knight, for democracy to thrive in an information era it is essential "to bestir the people into an awareness of their own condition, provide inspiration for their thoughts and rouse them to pursue their true interests."[17]

Chapter Nine

Law

Why Copyright and Privacy Matter So Much

*He who receives an idea from me, receives instruction
himself without lessening mine; as he who lights his
taper at mine, receives light without darkening me.*

—Thomas Jefferson, letter to Isaac McPherson, August 13, 1813

THE LAW IS a stumbling block on the route toward a
bright future for libraries. Many inspired, hardworking
librarians imagine a future in the digital age that is deeply
connected to the communities they serve. They have ambitious plans for how they might use digital tools to work in
partnership with schools, mentors, and prospective employ-
ers. But at the same time, they struggle with some of the most
basic tasks that a library has traditionally accomplished. That
struggle extends to lending books, movies, and music. In a
digital age, lending materials is much more complicated for
libraries than it was in the analog era. The law of copyright is

often blamed for this complication, but technological lock-down is part of the problem as well. Well-placed concerns about reader privacy also have the potential to slow down the transition to digital lending.

Most of the time, the law works as an enabling force in societies. When well designed, the law allows people to do things that they wish to accomplish. When the president of Harvard pronounces graduates of the law school, by tradition she says, "You are ready to aid in the shaping and application of those wise restraints that make men free." Much of the time, in a market-driven system, the law serves to make people free and operates in the background to enable fair and efficient marketplace activity.[1]

In other contexts, the law hinders progress, getting in the way when times have changed and not changing itself to keep up with altered market dynamics. A legislature might have established a delicate balance that made sense at one moment in history but no longer makes as much sense a few hundred years later. The law of copyright, which dates back to the founding of the United States (and beyond, to the Statute of Anne in early-eighteenth-century England), has become just such a hindrance when it comes to building strong libraries in a digital era. Librarians have been at the forefront of efforts to update the law to support their good works into the future.

Sensible copyright and privacy reforms are essential building blocks for libraries as they make the transition from the analog to the digital. Without changes to current law and policy, librarians will have a terribly hard time accomplishing their public-spirited mission in support of people living in a democracy. In fact, by standing in the way of librarians trying to take advantage of the ability to share knowledge more broadly, the law may lead instead to a backtracking from where we are today.

P UBLISHERS, EBOOK VENDORS, and libraries have spent the past few years engaged in a tug-of-war over the lending of electronic books. This clash inhibits most libraries from fulfilling their important institutional missions to provide access to knowledge and preserve our cultural heritage. In the best-case scenario, this tug-of-war will be a temporary struggle. If there must be a winner of any kind, it ought to be us, the reading public. Librarians need a team of allies pulling with them.[2]

A bit of background on the relevant law helps to set the scene for the tug-of-war. In the United States, copyright law grants to the creators of original works a bundle of *exclusive rights*—namely, the ability to exclude others, in the name of the law, from copying, adapting, distributing, displaying, or performing their creation. Should an individual (or a library, for that matter) make use of a copyrighted work in a manner that implicates one of these rights, an exception to the law must apply. Otherwise, the copyright owner may be able to make a successful claim for infringement.

Before e-readers and ebooks began their recent rise to popularity, libraries could acquire, lend, and preserve most copyrighted printed materials with relative ease. The only constraints were the size of their budgets, the space in their stacks, their time, and perhaps the interests of their patrons. For instance, libraries could easily add print materials to their collections that came in as donations (though, as any acquisitions librarian knows, donations are most often a mixed bag). Libraries could also make a limited number of digital copies of printed texts for the purposes of noncommercial lending and archiving, which helped to ensure that books that were badly damaged or no longer sold commercially were not lost to the public. Limitations in the Copyright Act enable these acts by libraries. Some of the law's provisions are omnibus in nature—meaning that they apply to everyone—and some apply specifically to libraries.

One of the limitations within copyright law that made book lending (and secondhand book sales) easy in the analog era is called the "first sale doctrine." Established in a landmark Supreme Court case in 1908 and formally codified in the Copyright Act in 1909, the first sale doctrine limits the copyright holder's right to distribution in a way that applies to everyone, not just libraries. The first sale doctrine states that the owner of a copy of a copyrighted work "is entitled, without the authority of the copyright owner, to sell or otherwise dispose of the possession of that copy." In plain English: copyright law only affords to the creator control of the *first sale* or distribution of a material copy of a work. Once a copy has been sold, the copyright owner can no longer stop that copy from being resold, lent, rented, or otherwise transferred to others. (Other rights still attach. For instance, the new owner of the book does not have the right to make a movie based on the book, which would violate another of the exclusive rights still held by the copyright holder.)

The first sale doctrine is the cornerstone that made possible secondary markets for copyrighted materials at video rental stores, used book and music stores, and libraries. In conjunction with other limitations in the Copyright Act, including "fair use" and other library-specific exceptions, the first sale doctrine enables libraries to build collections through donations, lend works to patrons, participate in interlibrary loan arrangements, and archive and preserve works for the benefit of future generations—all at minimal cost and without prior authorization from copyright owners. As the American Library Association puts it, "Quite simply, first sale is what allows libraries to do what we do—lend books and materials to our patrons, the public."[3]

The introduction of digital materials, particularly ebooks, has made things much more complex when it comes to libraries and lending. Other content industries have already had to deal with these changes; the shift from print to digital has disrupted the publishing industry, for instance, forcing publishers to adapt to a host of new media quickly. This transition has been no small feat, considering that publishing is an industry that has relied on the same basic models for centuries. The shift has highlighted the limitations of the US Copyright Act, which was designed to be applied in a world in which knowledge was recorded and then "fixed" (a key term in the copyright statute) in tangible, physical media. Much to the consternation of libraries and those they serve, these changes have caused publishers to rethink the business and legal structures that govern how they make works available—if at all—for library lending.

Print works are conventionally sold or donated to libraries. Invoking the first sale doctrine and other provisions under the law, libraries could lend their legally purchased print copies to patrons, to other libraries, and to the patrons of other libraries (through the extremely effective interlibrary loan systems). Digital works, in contrast, are typically licensed, not sold, to libraries and consumers. Licenses are enforceable contracts that grant permission to do or use something that otherwise would be the exclusive right of a property owner. The licenses offered by publishers to readers (or libraries) often contain additional terms and conditions that govern the scope and nature of the permission being granted. In the context of libraries, these terms and conditions (known as the "private law") might restrict, for instance, the ways in which libraries make works accessible to their patrons even if the background rules (known as the "public law") would allow it. Should the terms be violated, not only might the licensee lose the legal right to possess the work, but the licensor could seek recourse in court for a breach of contract. These licenses add restrictions on what can be done with the works that do not exist under copyright law.

This distinction between acquisitions and licensing of digital materials is not a new problem. Those who worry about copyrights have been arguing over this issue for more than thirty years. The same issue arises in the context of software and other forms of intellectual property. An ordinary user of software almost never "buys" it. As one walks out of Staples, one might hold a physical disk that has tax preparation software on it. The rights associated with this software, however, are defined not only by the copyright law—as they would be if one were walking out of a bookstore with a new hardcover—but also, and primarily, by the copy of a long, complicated license that has been shrink-wrapped into the package by the company that sold the software. This contract, some legal scholars argue, ends up trumping some of the rights that the public would otherwise enjoy to share or reuse the materials in various ways.

To envision the importance of this change for libraries, consider how the digital music world has changed over the past two decades. When one walked out of a record store with a new LP (a reference that will date any reader who recognizes this experience), the rights associated with that music were defined by the federal law of copyright. Among other things, the purchaser could sell that LP back to someone else—hence, secondhand record shops. In a world dominated by digital downloads, secondhand record shops have become endangered. The primary impediment for these shops is neither their historical problem of razor-thin margins nor the preference of young listeners to play music on digital devices. The problem is that the sale of a new song or album in a digital format comes with a license that commonly precludes resale. Movies that are streamed on demand are similarly constrained.

Libraries are not alone in bearing the brunt of these changes in how technology, the law, and user behaviors interact. Libraries are just the most recent case of acquirers who are becoming *renters,* not *owners,* of digital materials. The special problem in this instance is that libraries can be precluded from meeting one of their core obligations to the reading public: to lend them books, music, and movies to enjoy. The essential role for libraries of providing free access to culture to those who cannot otherwise afford it is in peril.

For libraries, the distinction between a license and a sale—the difference between renting and owning a copy of a work—is critical. The copyright holder maintains a stricter form of "ownership" of a licensed copy of a digital book—and much more control over what can be done with it—than in the case of an old-fashioned analog book. Put in more formal legal terms, there has been no transposition of the first sale doctrine into the digital sphere. As a result, the first sale doctrine probably does not apply to licensed copies. By definition, a digital book, sound recording, or image is not owned by the licensee. Libraries do not own their copies of ebooks, at least not in the same sense that they own their copies of printed books. The ability of libraries to provide their patrons with access to an ebook is conditional on their ability to adhere to the license terms.

As libraries consistently encounter license terms that prohibit or restrict their ability to provide core services to patrons, several concerns are raised for librarians. Will they be able to make copies of works for archival and format preservation purposes? Will licenses allow them to participate in interlibrary loan programs using digital works, or even print pages in some instances? Some ebook licenses expire after an ebook reaches a specified number of circulations, requiring the library to repurchase a costly license. This arrangement is plainly not as good for a library as being able to buy a print copy of a book outright in the first instance, presuming the book holds up reasonably well with use.

Like the law, technology can constrain as well as enable. Where license terms leave off, file formats can pick up with technological protections that govern—in the technical sense—how a work may be accessed and used through software and hardware. Although it is technically possible to overcome these technological measures (known as "digital rights management"), amendments to the Copyright Act in 1998 made it unlawful to circumvent such technological controls.[4]

At the same time, patron demand for ebooks is surging. The trend in favor of ebook reading is clear. Although the percentage of major publishers who offer lendable ebooks shows signs of improvement from a library patron's perspective, many publishers have simply refused to participate in lending programs or will only do so under a restrictive license. Libraries have had limited success in negotiating terms in their favor. License terms can supersede exceptions in the Copyright Act, including the very limitations on which libraries so heavily rely, and impose restrictions on the manner in which works may be accessed and used by patrons. The net effect is that a license allows for substantial control, particularly in cases where the licensee has little or no negotiating power.

These problems might be the temporary by-product of market growing pains, but many uncertainties remain for the growing volume of born-digital materials. Some libraries, especially children's and school libraries, rely heavily on book donations, which are made possible by the first sale doctrine. However, a licensed ebook is unlikely to be shareable with another library for lending purposes under current license terms. How will these libraries grow their digital collections? Even works in the public domain—works whose copyright terms have expired or to which no copyright was attached in the first place—may end up being produced as ebooks under onerous licenses or technical protection measures. If libraries are prohibited from preserving and archiving ebooks, copyrighted works may become orphans—works whose copyright owners become lost amid poor record-keeping, consolidation in the publishing industry, or bankruptcy.

Librarians and legal scholars have called on the courts and Congress for legislative reforms to rebalance the law to protect the interests of library users. For example, the Copyright Act could be amended simply to create a broad and effective "digital first sale" doctrine. In a more narrowly tailored fashion, Congress could provide libraries with special rights to ensure that they can lend, archive, and preserve ebooks. More expansively, Congress could implement a compulsory license system to cover digital lending through libraries whereby libraries and publishers would agree to royalty fees for ebooks. The legal system today might allow for readers and libraries to challenge the legality of particularly harmful licensing practices, like the contractual restrictions on fair use and the special exceptions granted to libraries; however, challenges of this sort can be long, expensive, and often inconclusive.

The judiciary could also take matters into its own hands. It is possible that one pending case in particular—called *Capitol Records v. ReDigi*—will have a transformative effect on how the first sale rule is interpreted by future courts in the digital environment. A start-up company called ReDigi has created a business model through which people can resell the digital music they have bought. Capitol Records sued ReDigi under the copyright statute, claiming that ReDigi's business model results in infringement of the copyrights that Capitol holds to sound recordings. A federal judge, Richard J. Sullivan, held in favor of Capitol Records on March 30, 2013, noting that "the Court cannot of its own accord condone the wholesale application of the first sale defense to the digital sphere, particularly when Congress itself has declined to take that step." ReDigi said it planned to appeal. The start-up has also announced its plans to move into the ebook space, which may soon provoke a showdown between it and book publishers analogous to its fight with Capitol Records.[5]

Beyond the legal options, the debate also presents opportunities for the creation of new business models that would satisfy both publishers and libraries. The good news is that this is a moment of substantial innovation in new business models and pilot programs that could generate profit for authors and publishers as well as access, through libraries, to the public. The American Library Association's Digital Content and Libraries Working Group is contributing important scholarship and open-minded thinking to help address this issue.[6]

Libraries, publishers, authors, and their agents should make common cause in conducting a series of experiments in ebook lending that could lead to a market-oriented solution. Creative ideas such as the "Buy-to-Unglue" project might play a role. In this crowdfunding model, every ebook purchase is counted toward a tally of sales. Once an ebook reaches a certain number of sold downloads, it becomes free to download for all subsequent readers, regardless of where they access the ebook. Such an approach could enable authors and publishers to establish a sales mechanism to reach a certain level of profitability before books become available for unlimited downloads through libraries, with print copies continuing to be sold.

A model for sustainable e-lending practices could take many forms. The simplest approach would be to mimic what happens in the analog world. If a library pays for a copy of a book, then the library owns that copy, whether it is analog or digital in form. Random House, one of the leading publishers, has adopted this policy. Other publishers fear that this policy will lead to diminished sales due to piracy, overlending, and a whole host of unknown concerns, and libraries fear it because, as long as no digital first sale doctrine is in place, they can have the digital books, but they're subject to onerous licenses.

A greater departure from the traditional lending model could benefit all parties. In a business model that allows for the pooling of funds from library acquisition budgets, a copyright holder could be paid according to the number of times the work is leant out by participating libraries. This model, often referred to as an "alternative compensation system," would come with many design challenges and risks, but over time it might lead to more revenue for booksellers from libraries, not less. Taking it a step further, a compulsory system could be set up to require that a copy be put on deposit for all forms of lending in exchange for the grant of a copyright from the government.[7]

National digital library initiatives might be another means to address the problem of copyright and ebook lending. The community that created the Digital Public Library of America could become an important force in collectively advocating on behalf of libraries and their readers. The national-level work to digitize and provide access to public domain works may have a substantial and positive effect over time. By starting with these openly accessible works, the DPLA seeks to ensure that access to them in digital form is maintained without license restrictions. The DPLA community is building a platform that will allow for experimentation. Alternative lending models might include lending digitized print books under copyright on a model championed by Brewster Kahle, the founder of the Internet Archive. Kahle argues forcefully that we need nothing more than the existing library rights in the Copyright Act to do much of what we need to do for readers. Open Library, a group of 150 participating libraries led by Kahle's Internet Archive, has set out to prove it through an initiative to partner with state libraries and others to digitize in-copyright words and lend them out one at a time.[8]

By working together on a public option, libraries can establish a public beachhead in the digital space dominated today by for-profits, including Amazon, Google, OverDrive, and commercial publishers. Those of us who care about libraries need to link arms in order to push back on law and technology trends that establish new restrictions on access rather than enabling increased access for a digital age. Otherwise, the digital age could perversely become an era with less accessibility, not more, than the analog age. Libraries should become more actively engaged in building the digital commons—through open-source code, open-access approaches to publishing, and innovative means of making copyrighted digital material available to readers.

THE EBOOK LENDING crisis takes on a further dimension in the global context. It is complicated enough to contemplate how US libraries will manage to lend digital materials subject to US copyright to readers based in the United States. Switch up any of these variables and the problem can get much harder. Libraries *outside* the United States may not be able to lend copyrighted materials from the United States to their reading publics at all under some licenses. Similarly, under French law, for instance, libraries in the United States may not be able to lend a copyrighted book that is governed by a restrictive license (under a "private law" arrangement). And the task of lending materials from a library in one jurisdiction to one in another jurisdiction is vastly more complex in a digital era than in the past, if not impossible.

Many European states are ahead of the United States, by a wide margin, in developing national digital library systems. In dozens of countries around the world, politicians have made commitments to create national digital libraries. The former president of France, Nicolas Sarkozy, pledged 750 million euros (equivalent at the time to US$1.1 billion) to digitize the "French patrimony."[9] Mr. Sarkozy's pledge was intended as a down payment on what French authorities thought was a total cost of roughly $1.5 billion to complete the mass digitization of the country's literary and archival works. The Scandinavian countries have also moved quickly to digitize collections in their highly effective national library systems, and the pan-European effort to draw these materials together, Europeana, draws connections across these state-based digital collections.[10]

Despite their head start in some related areas, Europeans are facing much the same conundrum as their counterparts in the United States. In the Netherlands, for example, librarians are struggling with a very similar e-lending situation. The Dutch library community is seeking to lend digital materials freely to the reading public, but recent legal opinions suggest that doing so may not be possible under Dutch law without additional licensing. State officials have promised to develop a national digital library, but a national-level solution appears to be a long way off. In the meantime, libraries are fretting about their ability to carry out their basic functions as reading patterns change.[11]

Among the countries that are furthest ahead in providing a national infrastructure for ebook lending is Singapore. Over 3 million ebooks are on offer there, and readers can borrow as many as eight digital titles from the national library system at once. Readership has been soaring: the number of ebook downloads rose from 3.9 million in the fiscal year ending in 2011 to 4.9 million the following year. Publishers and the library system have worked out a means to support at least some of the public demand for digital, in-copyright works at a national scale. Doing so in countries the size of the United States and in regions such as Europe is plainly more complicated, but the task is not impossible.[12]

A SECOND LEGAL CONUNDRUM, the orphan works problem, stands between libraries and a bright future in the digital-plus era. US copyright law has a strange provision that seems to benefit no one, and yet it persists. This part of the law speaks to whether it is lawful to share material whose copyright holder is unknown. This notion of "orphan works" might seem to be a small, esoteric matter. After all, don't most authors of books know that they hold the copyright?

As it turns out, there are millions of books and other materials from the twentieth century whose copyright holder is unknown.

The controversy surrounding orphan works has to do with whether a work of unknown copyright status should be treated as in-copyright or in a separate category. If an orphan work is treated as in-copyright and a library digitizes it and shares it with patrons in contravention of what the copyright holder might have wished, then the library could be liable for a high penalty—in the direst scenario, up to $150,000 per work under a statutory damages provision. The problem is that when a work is "orphaned," there is no "parent" from whom to get permission to digitize and share it. If the publisher or author doesn't exist or doesn't know that he or she is the copyright holder, there is no way for libraries to ask for and gain permission if they want to lend the work in this manner.

This orphan works problem is important because it could preclude the development of a massive digital library system. If there's no one who can approve the digitization and lending of a work, then the work is unlikely ever to be digitized and shared through a digital library system, nationally or globally. The law functions as a sword of Damocles swinging over the head of anyone who takes the risk of digitizing these orphan works without explicit permission. A graduate student researching education at the University of Alaska could easily find a digital version of a key book to help her complete her dissertation, but she is precluded from doing so if it cannot be digitized and made available to her. High school students studying fashion in twentieth-century America would benefit immensely from a digital archive of pattern books, even or maybe especially in cases where the owner is unknown, but they may never come across these vital resources. No one benefits from the current law—most especially students.

The orphan works problem would not be so important to resolve if the number of works involved were smaller, but in fact the number of such works is vast. Estimates place it in the millions in the United States alone, and millions more across the world. John Wilkin, director of the HathiTrust project, estimates that as many as half of the works in the HathiTrust corpus are orphans, amounting to 2.5 million as of 2011. Another report "conservatively" estimates that the combined research institutions of the United Kingdom hold more than 50 million orphan works.[13]

The current legal status of orphan works serves no one. The fear associated with changing the law is expressed by those who purport to represent copyright holders. These opponents of change in the law wish to preserve the ability to sue libraries if aggrieved copyright holders can be found. This logic, however, is weak. The law could easily allow for previously orphaned works to revert to copyright status upon a successful showing from copyright holders of their rights in the work. At that point, the libraries that were sharing the digital copy of the work would have to treat it as though it were any other in-copyright work. Indeed, making the works available would almost certainly lead to more accurate assignments of copyright interests as old works are surfaced and made relevant to readers. They might come to the attention of not only the public but also the rightful copyright holders. There is also no reason why libraries couldn't get special dispensation of this sort under the law if broader reform of orphan works failed to attract enough votes.

Copyright holders also express a fear that reform of the law will somehow cause a loss of revenue if orphaned works are treated as distinct from in-copyright works. This concern also seems misplaced. The works in question have next to no commercial value. Works that have been orphaned have long since stopped being sold to anyone for any purpose. The desire of libraries to digitize and share them while they have orphan status is intended to render them potentially useful to the extraordinarily small number of readers who might chance upon them and find them of interest—most likely, those who would put them to a scholarly or esoteric personal use. Again, if an orphaned work is determined to have an active copyright holder, the work would revert to full copyright status and could then be exploited as a work of commercial value—if in fact it has some.

The important step in legal reform of the copyright law with respect to orphan works is to make sure that creative works can be accessed and enjoyed. This type of reform would be wholly consistent with the original Copyright Act, which was intended to strike a bargain between the interests of creators in making a reasonable profit and the right of the public to engage with creative works. The current law with respect to orphan works accomplishes neither goal. A new author or creator does not have an added incentive to write or create because, when orphaned, her work could not be digitized and shared broadly. And the current law sets a major disincentive in place for libraries to digitize and share these many works with the small audiences who might wish to enjoy them.

Within the library community there is a split between those who favor a push toward orphan works legislation and those who dislike the law but wish to keep things as they are. Many who care about libraries fear that opening up the copyright law right now with the current Congress, which has proved hostile to many library interests and friendly to large copyright holders, would result in a law that is less favorable rather than more favorable. After all, under the current system libraries or others can digitize orphan works and make them available to the public—they just run the risk of a lawsuit if they do so. A rational court system might hold in their favor if a challenge to the library's actions were to be brought, thereby potentially clearing the way for mass digitization of orphan works. Though suboptimal from a public policy viewpoint, this self-help approach—despite the risks inherent to libraries—might be the best way forward for the time being. Either way, orphan works should be digitized and made easily available to the public, at least unless and until a copyright holder is identified.

A final potential copyright reform that would favor libraries and mass digitization is change to the part of the law that relates specifically to libraries. Known as Section 108, this provision allows libraries to do specific things that other institutions cannot do. For example, it enables libraries to make copies of works that they own for preservation purposes. The Copyright Act also allows libraries to make works available to the blind and others with disabilities, in a range of formats. The Section 108 protections and other special exemptions that libraries can take advantage of to meet their goals are sensible so far as they go, but they are limited. They function as a "safe harbor" in which libraries can take on certain functions that might otherwise violate someone's copyright interests, but where the public interest trumps these private interests.

A movement to reform Section 108 in the past decade drew together major figures from the library world, who came up with sensible recommendations to improve the law for the digital era. Their suggestions went nowhere. The past several US Congresses have not discussed or advanced meaningful library reform proposals.

A copyright law should include a stronger set of provisions to protect libraries from liability as they meet their public-spirited goals in the digital age. These reforms could take the form of improvements to the federal copyright law, sound opinions by courts in interpreting key provisions of the law (especially the fair use exception), or a combination of legislative and judicial actions. In the meantime, libraries, archives, and other cultural heritage institutions must continue to make their way with some of their most important activities shrouded in uncertainty. Librarians must run some risk as they go forward, in the spirit of both meeting their core goals and improving the law as they do so.

L IBRARIANS LOVE TO quote Supreme Court Justice Louis Brandeis: "The right to be left alone—the most comprehensive of rights, and the right most valued by a free people."[14] Privacy is a simpler topic than copyright when it comes to ebooks and lending, though no less important. For many years, librarians have been the leading voices in public debates about individual privacy, and in fact, librarians may be society's most effective privacy advocates. In the digital era, librarians face new challenges when it comes to upholding a strict level of privacy protections for readers.[15]

The problem of reader privacy, much like copyright, is encapsulated in the distinction between books that are acquired and those that are licensed. In the analog world, when a book is acquired by a library, no further relationship is required between the library and anyone involved in the production of the book. The library pays the cost of the book, puts it into the collection, and then lends it out to whomever first comes asking for it. The library may keep a record of who has the book in order to ensure that all books don't go permanently missing or to assess fines, but the library can apply its own standards to the question of how those data are used.

In a digital world, the transaction between the library and the publisher or provider of the work is more complex. The transaction ordinarily comes with "strings attached," which are articulated in the form of license terms. As we have seen in the context of copyright, the library is paying for a license to a work—if it can get such a license—that enables it to lend the work to a patron. But the library is probably not doing the lending in the literal sense. The publisher may have worked with a company, such as the market-leading Over-Drive, to enable the lending of an ebook to a library patron. Or perhaps a publisher has established a means of enabling direct loans to patrons, with the library merely paying the fees. In these cases, the librarian is relying on the third parties or the publisher to protect user privacy in the ways that librarians have done in the past.

A profit-led approach may work out just fine from a user privacy perspective, but it is risky. Companies that serve libraries will no doubt be aware of the fierce commitment to reader privacy that librarians bring to their work. The market may well function in a manner that benefits readers: companies that manage e-lending processes will want to attract librarians as customers for their services and will therefore establish practices that favor individual privacy over other interests. Companies that fail to protect user privacy will find libraries dropping their services quickly and in droves. Unfortunately, as we have seen time and again, the market does not always function perfectly, especially when it comes to user privacy.

This state of affairs makes some librarians understandably nervous. Whereas librarians were once in control of information related to their patrons' reading patterns, today they are being cut out of that central role. In the digital world, libraries are being "disintermediated" at various crucial turns, which is to say that they are no longer the essential intermediary between people and information. The key intermediaries in the e-lending environment are increasingly for-profit firms, which may do the right thing, but may also be swayed by interests other than long-standing library values, such as reader privacy, as their services evolve over time.

Librarians worry, with some reason, about what protections readers will have when the police come calling for information about the books they have checked out. Librarians have long fought encroachments on civil liberties of this sort. The debate over the USA Patriot Act was a major cause célèbre for librarians, for instance. The notion that a reader's interest in a book about Islam might tip an investigation toward a particular suspect sent chills down the collective spines of librarians. Their fear is justified: for-profit firms may not stand as firm as libraries would in the face of state pressure.

THE CHALLENGES OF the digital era for libraries can be addressed in part through smart legal reforms. An enlightened Congress could take a look at the entire set of library-related statutes, including those related to copyright and privacy, and make updates that would serve the reading public well and enable libraries to thrive in the future. But most people involved in libraries fear opening such a discussion today. The faith of the public in Congress is so low, and the concern about achieving worse outcomes rather than improvements is so great, that the prospect of such a grand discussion seems unlikely at best. A better bet would be that libraries and publishers will team up to solve the e-lending crisis in the near term.

Librarians must continue to be among those leaders who step up to the challenge of fixing our copyright and privacy laws. Whether through the private ordering done in back-room deals or in the public arena, we need our librarians to lead the way. Too few people give voice to the public interest, and the world of knowledge and information is becoming increasingly controlled by corporations. Just as we, the public, need to make the case for libraries, we all need the library profession to help make the case for a sensible, public-friendly copyright and privacy regime for the digital era.

Chapter Ten

Conclusion

What's at Stake

Knowledge is in every country the surest basis of public happiness.

—George Washington, First Annual Message to Congress
on the State of the Union, January 8, 1790

WHEN ASKED WHAT they like best about libraries, people often recall browsing in dimly lit stacks for a book. The browsing experience is one of the most magical childhood memories for many people. They have positive associations with the experience of tracking down a book by call number, wending their way through the aisles, and running their finger along the spines of books in musty library stacks. The joy of unexpected discovery has enormous appeal to people of all ages and all walks of life.

The library browsing experience is strongly associated with the concept of serendipity. There is something powerful about the idea that patrons will find on the shelves books that they didn't expect to find. To date, this experience has come about thanks to the physical proximity of other books to the book they are initially seeking. For some people, it is impossible to come out of the stacks without armfuls of books, even if they went into the stacks seeking just one. This serendipity has broader social implications too. New ideas and new connections between fields can be created as a result of these unexpected findings. This serendipity, this sense of discovery, relies on a long and complex chain of activities, many of them carried out by librarians.

There is reason to fear that this type of positive experience will be lost if library stacks, and the people who staff them, disappear. If libraries shed their physical collections and materials are rendered to patrons through electronic delivery only, the experience of serendipity could be lost forever. The same fear goes for the decline of the physical, printed newspaper. When a reader searches only for a narrow topic and ends up with a single story, she may miss the surrounding stories that offer a broader snapshot of what's happening in the world. (Even the prospect of moving previously inaccessible stacks can lead to public outcry, as occurred with the New York Public Library in 2012.)

If libraries were to disappear, cities and towns would lose essential "third places" that are open to the public. In a 2013 survey, 90 percent of Americans age sixteen and older said that the closing of their local public library would have a negative impact on their community. There are many sound reasons for this concern. Outside of home and work, third places in many communities are shifting away from library spaces and toward commercial spaces, whether Starbucks in the physical world or Facebook in the virtual world. The fate of many of America's Carnegie libraries brings this fear into relief. Built early in the twentieth century, hundreds of the original Carnegie libraries have now been either closed or renovated for entirely different purposes; in either event, they no longer meet the information needs of their communities in the ways that they once did. Without the public spaces that libraries provide, the most vulnerable people in our society will not have safe, comfortable places to go to access information, think, write, and learn.[1]

We should fear the impact on our education system of closing library branches and shortening hours at those that remain open. There is good reason to worry that the ability of a community's young people to learn, to search for and discover information, and to sort credible information from less credible information will be diminished if the community's library services are reduced. Students are using Google in particular, as well as other web-based services, but without a great deal of sophistication. The library's role in the learning process is being displaced by commercial outfits (think of Amazon and its recommendations) and highly distributed nonprofits (think of Wikipedia).

We also have reason to worry about losing important parts of the record of our shared history. Right now, digital materials are harder than physical materials to preserve. Without libraries acquiring books, manuscripts, newspapers, and other materials and holding on to them for posterity, we stand to lose more than we gain from the digital transformation in terms of long-term preservation. Librarians and archivists fear, with good reason, that scholars today are preserving much less of their work than in the past: with email and web-based publication, notes made as Word documents, and so forth, they worry that materials that once were routinely set aside for the future will not be preserved. The prospect of our shared history being less well preserved in the digital world than in the analog world would be a perverse—and avoidable—outcome of the "information revolution."

Libraries and archives that are open and free to all provide essential services to the public every day. As systems and as networks, these institutions provide equally important long-term services to democracies as they decide which texts and images to hold for posterity and which to let fade away, to become ephemeral. Today's task is to preserve the most important aspects of libraries while taking advantage of what can now be accomplished in a digital era—all at a moment when public resources for libraries appear to be on the wane.

MARILYN JOHNSON WROTE a book about libraries and librarians that I love called *This Book Is Overdue!* In the concluding line of her introduction, Johnson writes: "So where does one go in such a wobbly, elusive, dynamic, confusing age? Wherever the librarians and archivists are. . . . They're sorting it all out for us."[2]

Other observers of libraries agree with Ms. Johnson's rosy outlook for libraries in the digital era. In an optimistic piece in the Huffington Post, the entrepreneur and author Jeanniey Mullen writes:

Today's libraries have risen to a new level. They are striving to be more than a resource or lending institution. They are evolving into market leaders and trend-setters, all while offering digital services like eBooks, educational databases and job assistance programs that help their communities. When the world continues to become more global and digital, many libraries are finding ways to maintain a personal and local approach that ensures every neighborhood can explore globally while residing locally.[3]

Though I admire their sense of optimism and enjoy their writing, I am not so sanguine as Johnson and Mullen about the future of libraries. Some librarians and archivists *are* sorting out the future for us. Some librarians are market leaders and trend-setters. They are certainly pointing the way, much as library leaders in great city libraries like Boston, New York, Chicago, and San Francisco are doing, and librarians in many small-town libraries as well. They are the wonderful people I've written about in this book, including Annemarie Naylor in Colchester, England; Melissa Techman in Albemarle County, Virginia; Nate Hill in Chattanooga, Tennessee; Kari Lämsä in Helsinki, Finland; Matthew Winner in Ellicott City, Maryland; Luis Herrera in San Francisco; and many other leaders.

But these positive assessments are not universally true, nor do they tell the entire story. There are too many librarians and archivists who are wringing their hands rather than putting those hands to work and collaborating to build a positive version of the digital future. More important, many other people are working hard—frankly, often harder and more productively than the library community—on related problems. Technologists, publishers, authors, agents, business strategists—all are working on the same set of problems, from different angles. There's a great deal of innovation going on around the world outside of the United States library scene, and we need to incorporate it into the operations of our libraries and archives.

My primary fear about the future of libraries—and this is where I part company with Johnson—is that those in the for-profit sector are working much more quickly and effectively to address many of these same problems, only with a profit motive rather than the public interest as their driver. And they have much more capital and talent devoted to the task.

Right now, I'd put much greater odds on the programmers and graphic designers at Amazon, Apple, and Google than I would on those in the library community to figure out the next big thing in information and knowledge management. Although there have been, and are, inspiring pioneers in the nonprofit space—Brewster Kahle of Internet Archive, Carl Malamud at public.resource.org, Sue Gardner and Jimmy Wales at the Wikimedia Foundation, Mitchell Baker and her crew at Mozilla, and the late Aaron Swartz all jump to mind—they are often not seen, much less welcomed, as part of the library movement or profession. There are fabulous theorists and doers dreaming up the future of the library world. Dan Cohen, Robert Berring, Robert Darnton, Lorcan Dempsey, Peter Morville, Jenny Levine, Peter Suber, David Weinberger, Jessamyn West, and too many others to list here have written influential work about libraries, their futures, and how to innovate our way there. As forceful as the ideas of these leaders are, the for-profit sector has far more resources backing their ideas for innovation than the library sector. There is a massive research-and-development gap between libraries and others who are seeking to solve similar problems.

There are simply too few people within libraries right now who are working on highly innovative digital projects that could have a positive impact at scale. As budgets are stretched and libraries are forced to meet demands in both the analog and digital worlds, library leaders are hard-pressed to invest in pure innovation or R&D work. And there are too few partnerships between libraries and other types of organizations— for instance, Microsoft Research, Cisco's global R&D team, or Google's nonprofit arms—that could bear enormous fruit in the public interest. Libraries could use a twenty-first-century Andrew Carnegie to invest in the digital equivalent of the Carnegie libraries of the analog era.[4]

Even if we came up with the resources as societies, librarians are often too fearful to take risks. An innovative librarian from Finland, Kari Lämsä, said it well in an interview: "Libraries are not so serious places. We should not be too afraid of mistakes. We are not hospitals. We cannot kill people here. We can make mistakes and nobody will die. We can try and test and try and test all the time." A spirit of risk-taking and assessment, so common among technology developers, has an important place in the world of libraries today.

Those of us who care deeply about the future of libraries are too likely to rely on the deep nostalgia about libraries rather than take risks and invest now in a bright future. The temptation to rely on nostalgia is understandable. Survey after survey, anecdotal encounter after anecdotal encounter, shows us that people "love libraries." Just as we all love a *memory* of a childhood experience, we love the *idea* of libraries in general. Often, it feels like a patronizing sort of love. An approach that relies too heavily on nostalgia to pull libraries as institutions through this period of transformational change is a dangerous one. It could work, but it is too risky. It is ultimately a losing strategy.

Libraries have underinvested in R&D during a period when the field of information has undergone radical change. Library funds for technology have gone primarily to pay vendors, usually for-profits, for new products that have automated library services. These funds have been well spent, by and large, and the for-profit field of vendors has done important, positive things for libraries. The most important library consortia and nonprofits—including the Online Computer Library Center, the Council on Library and Information Resources, and ITHAKA—have made large contributions to library innovation. But the overall amount spent by libraries to refurbish how they operate pales in comparison to what is spent on search, discovery, and e-commerce in Silicon Valley. It is no surprise that students are turning less and less frequently to librarians for support. A concerted push toward innovation, fueled by librarians themselves, in partnership with those who specialize in information technologies, could pay enormous benefits. This R&D should promote new methods of both access and long-term preservation.

Physical libraries and digital libraries will continue to coexist, certainly for the foreseeable future and perhaps forever. Greater investment in library research and development could help to translate the best of the physical library world into the digital. For instance, experimentation in digital browsing could eliminate the problem of reduced serendipity with the removal of physical stacks. Indeed, stacks created in virtual space could be far more effective than physical stacks, which are limited to the physical objects present in a particular physical space. A library patron walking down a single aisle of a single branch library in Chicago can see far fewer books than that same patron could see browsing online, looking at a virtual set of stacks that combine all the books in the main library and all the branches. She would not smell the must on the books or be able to touch the spines, but using a virtual browsing method, she might find more, not less, than she would in a physical set of stacks. The innovators at the Harvard Library Innovation Lab have created just such a virtual browsing engine. Called StackView, it is free and open—much like the great public libraries.[5]

This stepped-up investment in library R&D should support the creation of open-source systems and open-access materials that can be used and reused by any library. The design question that should animate these systems is whether there are ways to use the online environment, either on its own or in combination with the physical environment, to ensure that the positive associations with libraries—learning, discovery, good feelings—are not lost. In fact, it might be possible to do better, not worse, on this front in a digital-plus world, where materials are created digitally and then rendered in a variety of digital and analog formats for different readers. Library R&D is necessary if librarians are to determine means of ensuring the long-term preservation of born-digital materials, especially those that are at enormous scale, that are interactive, or that are designed to change over time.

Library R&D is also needed to ensure that all citizens benefit from the digital revolution, and enhanced library R&D ought to be especially focused on the work of making digital materials available to people with various physical disabilities. Digital works can be made to be read to those who cannot see or to appear in much larger print for those whose sight requires it. Today some books appear in these digitally enhanced formats, but many do not, and many people with vision difficulties do not have consistent access to these types of works. To date, we have invested too little as a society in ensuring that the gap between the digital haves and have-nots does not grow along lines of different basic human capabilities.

The other necessary area of increased investment is in the training and retraining of librarians and library students. Especially during this time of transition, libraries have spent far too little on professional development. Librarians have much to teach one another; in fact, the most digitally savvy librarians are some of the most digitally savvy professionals anywhere. The great desire of librarians to learn and to hone their craft, recognizing full well that the expectations of those they serve are changing, should be met by library leaders' equally strong commitment to pay consistently for more training.

T HE TIME HAS come to pursue a new strategy for libraries that will shape, rather than merely react to, the digital revolution. Librarians and archivists need support as they develop a more coordinated and effective system that can bridge the analog and the digital in democratic societies. This strategy is well on its way to being implemented, but in uncoordinated and spotty ways. As the science fiction writer William Gibson put it, "The future is here—it's just not very evenly distributed yet." The need for collective action, both to define and to build an enhanced system of libraries for the digital age, is great.[6]

Through a grand bargain, we can—and must—set libraries on a sustainable path for the future. As the public, we need to invest more, not less, in libraries during this period of transition. The two areas most desperately in need of more funding are research and development and professional development,

even as librarians continue their shift toward digital, collaborative, and networked activities.

As part of the grand bargain, librarians and publishers
need to work together to develop one or more models for
sustainable e-lending practices. Just as it is important for libraries to thrive, other parts of the information ecosystem
need to thrive too. Publishers, authors, editors, and agents
ought to be able to make an honest profit from books and
other copyrighted materials. The remaking of libraries should
enable reasonable forms of ebook lending, but need not eliminate payments for works; copyright holders ought to be able
to make a fair and sustainable profit. And Google and Amazon should not be the only beneficiaries of the digital transition. The reading public needs to be the ultimate beneficiary.

In this new world, libraries and librarians will take on
additional tasks that are needed to support democratic institutions. Libraries will be working in closer collaboration
with other partners and sometimes delegating tasks to other
libraries and consortia that were previously done in-house.
As the library-using public, we need to be willing to accept
lower levels of service in traditional areas during this period
of transition.

Considering how much we would all miss the loss of quiet
reading rooms and overfilled stacks if they were to go away,
the best approach would be for communities to decide to pay
for the wonderful old analog services and spaces as well as the
new digital-era services. If every library budget—whether in a
public, school, or academic setting—were to rise to meet the

new costs as well as all of the old, we would surely all benefit. A world of greatly expanded funding for libraries, however, enough to cover the old and the new, seems unthinkable today. Nevertheless, librarians should ask for more funding, and we as communities should provide it. If a trade-off is necessary between the old-fashioned and the new-fangled— which seems likely—our inclination must be toward the future for libraries.

Libraries must continue to make the shift toward the digital and away from print. The shift should not be overnight, but it should be made steadily and with great care. Libraries can and should de-accession physical materials much more aggressively than they do today, especially to save space and money when these materials are redundant with other local collections or digital forms of access to them. The public will have to accept slower delivery times for print-related materials to come back from efficient shared storage facilities.

As libraries continue to de-emphasize physical collections, they will ramp up services associated with finding, using, and co-creating digital materials. They will continue to provide contemplative public spaces and uplifting, informative programming that people can't find elsewhere. They will find ways to meet the learning needs of both our ablest students and our neediest students.

Libraries should continue the positive trend toward collaboration on preservation tasks in order to achieve the goal of long-term archiving and storage of materials. Such collaboration needs to be much more systematic and consistent than it is today. The net effect will be improvements in techniques for digital preservation as they become more effective, cheaper, and more reliable over time. Print collections will be retained as long-term backup and for usage by those who prefer print, but patrons will have to wait longer for printed materials to show up than they will for digital versions, which can be more efficiently procured.

This grand bargain will require sacrifices on all sides. Librarians will need to stop doing many of the chores associated primarily with acquiring and managing their print collections and start doing others. Patrons will need to accept certain inconveniences, such as longer wait times if they wish to access print versions of materials. The important core activities of libraries, however, will persist: providing continuous access to, and context for, the knowledge that people need in order to thrive in a democracy, now and over the long term.

How should we pay for this expensive transition? The legacy of library philanthropists, including Joshua Bates in Boston and Andrew Carnegie across the nation, casts a long shadow. The positive effects of what their investments catalyzed are felt every day, both in communities in the United States and around the world. Public libraries provide access to materials and services that were unthinkable at the founding of the American Republic, yet have become an essential part of making our democracy work.

These early philanthropists and their gifts remain controversial to this day. Some worry about accepting "tainted money" from rapacious capitalists to pay for public goods. Others fear the impact of the paternalism of the wealthy on our cities and towns. Some librarians have long disliked aspects of the designs that Carnegie insisted upon.

Whatever its shortcomings, however, the massive public and private investment in the library system at the end of the nineteenth century and the beginning of the twentieth was an enormously positive event for American democracy and economic growth. This investment made good on the promise of each individual's ability to pursue his or her own true interests in a free and open society. Shelves of books that were once closed—as was deemed best even by the great librarian Melvil Dewey as late as 1877—became open to all citizens. The system of public libraries would not have come together in such a sweeping way without the generosity of people who believed in this ideal and were willing to pay the bill for the capital costs. These capital gifts came with strings attached that proved very effective. For instance, towns that accepted the Carnegie gifts had to commit to taxing themselves at a rate of 10 percent of the original gift to pay for upkeep of the building, books, and library staff salaries.[7]

The moment is right for a new investment of this same type and scale. The libraries that were built a hundred years ago were designed for a different information world. Libraries today need a capital infusion to support innovation, development of a common digital platform, training and retraining of library staff, and creation of systems of digital distribution that will work well for society at large. If we fail to make this capital investment in public-spirited libraries in the near term in support of a dramatic transition, our democracies will suffer. As Walter Cronkite said, "Whatever the cost of our libraries, the price is cheap compared to that of an ignorant nation."[8]

L IBRARIANS MUST CREATE new nostalgia. The purpose of renewed investment in libraries should be to establish new services and ways of discovering and accessing knowledge. At a minimum, the investment that is needed is a capital infusion—both from philanthropists and from the state—into libraries that will pay for both librarian training in new technological skills and the development of digital platforms on the scale of Carnegie's investments in the physical infrastructure of libraries.

This innovation must not be left to the for-profit sector alone. Great companies that serve libraries among others (such as Innovative Interfaces) and historically important nonprofit consortia (such as OCLC) should both play a big role in this redefinition of libraries. A few huge libraries have set up terrific research and development operations; the NYPL Labs, for instance, are the self-described "digital skunk works at The New York Public Library." But these innovative efforts are few and far between and underfinanced. More people working on the front lines in all kinds of libraries— school, public, research, government, special collections— should be directly engaged in this process of reinvention, with the goal of serving the general interest, not developing a new product to market.

Those familiar with Internet-speak will immediately recognize the acronym OBE. It means "overtaken by events." In ordinary usage, it indicates that a delayed email reply is no longer needed or relevant ("Thanks, but that's OBE"). My fear is that libraries will be perceived, wrongly, as OBE if we don't act together to help with the transition to the digital-plus era. If my fear is misplaced, that would be terrific. But it would be much smarter for libraries, and those who love them, to participate in the process of redefining libraries.

The end result of this redefinition will not, and should not, be all about the digital. I expect that it will result in a powerful *reaffirmation* of the importance of physical spaces in libraries, for a wide variety of good reasons. Just as there is a need for those in the nonprofit sector to take part in the innovation of libraries and information services, there is a deep need in society for public spaces—digital and physical spaces that are not owned by companies. Libraries are perfectly suited to play this essential cultural and social role, in ways that are distinct from a general community center model. And building on the vast and enduring credibility they enjoy as a profession, librarians are perfect for this role. Librarians are deeply trustworthy, for good reason.

SINCE I HAVE advanced an argument that runs throughout this book, it seems only fair to take up a few of the many counterarguments to my position in favor of meaningful reinvestment, by the state and by private philanthropy, in libraries. The primary counterargument is the straw man

against which my argument is set: the premise that we somehow need libraries less in a digital era than we did in an analog era. For all the reasons I've stated so far, I think that this
argument is not only wrong but dangerous for leaders in a
democratic system to adopt. Libraries serve essential functions even in a world in which we can rely on Google, Facebook, and Twitter for answers to many of life's questions. A
library's functions may be different in nature than they once
were, but the core elements of the library mission from past
centuries, providing broad access and consistent preservation, remain deeply important today.

An additional counterargument is that my thesis in fact
does not go far enough. Some futurists contend that the
digital era is upon us and that the measured approach that
I suggest, pivoting from the analog to the digital, is insuffi-
ciently bold. This counterargument calls for a faster move
to the cloud-based, all-digital future that could lead to un-
told innovation and improvements in human knowledge.
The move to shutter physical libraries is sound, the argument
goes, not because we can't afford them and should use the
money for fire and police departments instead, but because
the money should be put toward further innovation in information technologies, whether in libraries or otherwise, in the
name of competitiveness. A variant of this counterargument
is that the market will take care of this transition on behalf of
the public. Critics taking this libertarian line contend that I
am too quick to write off the value of innovations in search,
discovery, and preservation devised by the for-profit sector.

This counterargument about the rate of change and who should lead it is the one that is least compelling to me. There is much to love about today's libraries, and good reason not to dismantle them quickly in the name of innovation. We need for libraries to invest in their people and in common technological infrastructure, but not at the expense of quiet reading rooms, services for new immigrants and job seekers, and public learning spaces for children in our cities and towns. We need to have a period of transition from a predominantly analog to a predominantly digital world that is orderly and gradual, not abrupt. Many librarians are doing a good job of managing this transition; they should be supported as they try to persuade their colleagues and be given time to manage the change in a sustainable fashion. The end of this transition should find local branch libraries, great research libraries, and school libraries still in place, both as physical spaces and as service centers that provide enormous direct benefits to the people they serve. Digital innovation must happen, and it will, but too great a rush to change will break down too much in libraries that is of value, too quickly. I favor a hybrid of the virtual and the analog, the strong middle course that falls between the "if it ain't broke don't fix it" approach and the "let's get on with the change more quickly" argument.

And then there is the counterargument that I, as a nonlibrarian, am not the one who should be saying what librarians should or shouldn't do. I am especially sensitive to this criticism. As a library director without a library degree, I came in for a lot of criticism from librarians who felt

I shouldn't have been appointed to the job I had. These concerns were broached on listservs and on public blogs, a pile of which well-meaning people forwarded along to me to see. When the DPLA announced the appointment of a highly qualified nonlibrarian as its founding executive director, a similar set of criticisms made the rounds. Some librarians are wary of "ferals." In a moment of crisis for a field, when many people worry about whether they will be able to keep their jobs, I can understand this concern.

Especially during this time of transition, the library community ought to be open to those in other fields who share similar goals and who support the important functions that libraries serve. The library ethos in favor of intellectual freedom, the public exchange of ideas, and the pursuit of the truth should trump the impulse to protectionism. Part of operating as a network involves connecting to those from other fields with something to offer. The argument that I advance in this book might be wrong, and no doubt can be improved through dialogue. But it is grounded in a genuine desire to be a part of the movement to promote libraries in a digital era, and that must be a collaborative effort, engaging both librarians and nonlibrarians, in order to be successful.

HERE IS A specific path forward, in ten steps, for all of us who care about libraries, now and into the future:

1. We must redefine libraries for a digital-plus era and recast them as platforms. By "digital-plus" I mean that

materials are born digital and then rendered in a variety of formats, some print (traditional books and hard copies of images) and some digital (ebooks, interactive games, image files, audio and visual works in digital format). By "platforms" I mean that libraries should function as nodes in a highly networked digital world rather than as discrete and sometimes even competitive entities.

2. Libraries must act as ambitiously networked institutions. They need to be able to operate at scale and to put scale to good use for patrons. Libraries must connect their network effectively with partner institutions: archives, historical societies, museums, and other cultural heritage organizations.

3. The basis of this redefinition must be demand-driven, firmly grounded in what people and communities need from libraries today and in the future, not in nostalgia for how things may or may not have really been in the past. Aligning with community needs will help ease libraries' money problems, insofar as they will be better able to make the case that they are helping to solve their community's problems—witness how successfully Brian Bannon and his team made this case in Chicago, garnering Mayor Rahm Emanuel's enthusiastic support.

4. In the process of redefining libraries, we must account for both the physical and the analog. There is a place for both in the library of the future, whether in formats for materials, spaces, or experiences for patrons.

5. Librarians should only seek to do those things that need doing and take advantage of areas in which libraries have comparative advantage in serving the public interest.

6. Librarians should seek common cause with authors, agents, editors, and publishers. Libraries exist as part of an ecosystem of knowledge creators. The roles of some of these players may change, but their functions remain valuable.

7. Certain library spaces should function more like labs, or "co-production facilities," where people interact with information and make new knowledge. Instead of remaining what was known as "laboratories for books" at the end of the nineteenth century, when books served as the raw materials for scholarly inquiry, libraries should be laboratories for a digital-plus era in which co-production is the norm.

8. Librarians should work together, in common cause with technologists, to create a shared, open digital infrastructure, at scale, and then build from there. They should draw upon hacker culture and the lessons of the creation of the Internet in creating this digital infrastructure, in which we need to invest vastly more capital and time than we do today.

9. Preservation of knowledge needs to become far more of a collaborative task than it is today. Libraries should maintain physical spaces, but use them for lots of purposes other than the storage of physical materials. We

are radically underinvesting in the task of long-term digital preservation.

10. We need to be willing to pay for the transition of libraries into this new era, much as philanthropists, communities, and universities stepped up in the late nineteenth and early twentieth centuries. These capital costs, plowed into library R&D geared toward both access and preservation, will pay great dividends in the form of democratic returns.

The net result of rethinking libraries as institutions, and the role of librarians as professionals, will be a balance between the traditional and the innovative. The most visionary librarians have sought to strike this balance for a long time. The historical principles of librarianship—universal access to information, individual privacy, freedom of expression, and truth above all else—are as necessary now as they have ever been and must persist. At the same time, the balance of library leadership needs to swing more forcefully toward the new or libraries will fade in their significance to the American public. Libraries are not alone in needing to find this balance. Schools and newspapers, for instance, are facing similar moments of crisis and reinvention and have a central role to play in charting the future. Each of these institutions plays a role in informing, educating, and engaging the public in our common interest. We need to get it right in all three cases.

The most promising development in the world of libraries is the growth of innovative systems that enable libraries to function as a network rather than as stand-alone institutions. Elements of this network have been either in place or in development for a long time. The human part of the network—the librarians themselves—have been finding ways to collaborate in effective ways. The addition of high-speed network access to many libraries around the world has established a fantastic technical network. The third piece that is coming together now is the set of skilled librarians who know how to make the most of these networks. They know how to leverage social networks, open-source platforms, and open-access materials in ways that matter for library patrons today and in the future. The net result will be local institutions that are better able to meet immediate patron demands as well as engage in large-scale collaborations that will meet the long-term needs of the library field and of society at large.

Without greater public support, librarians will not be in a position to make this switch to the networked, collaborative modes of operating that hold such promise. All of us, whether individual citizens or institutional leaders, need to devote more capital and time, especially during this transitional period, to supporting libraries as they make these changes. Libraries need to be able to draw on more than nostalgia in order to make the case for the increased investment of public and private resources. This is a bargain well worth making, one that is true to the original mission of public libraries.

Why must these services be provided by public institutions and not the private sector? The notion of a true "public option" is central to my argument—just as it was in

Boston and elsewhere in the middle of the nineteenth century. When it comes to the knowledge and information on which our system of democracy depends, we should not rely on the market exclusively to meet the needs of our communities. The private sector has been wildly successful in digital innovation, and in some areas, such as the supply of corporate email systems, it has been just fine for the private sector to lead. When it comes to the cultural, historical, political, and scientific record of a society, however, the public sector needs to play a leading role. In the near term, that role involves providing unbiased, even-handed, universal access to the knowledge needed to be a good citizen and to thrive in an increasingly information-based economy. In the long term, that role involves preserving the record against the inevitable ravages of time, whether in the form of fire, technological change, political spite, or other threats to the preservation of important materials.

It is not too much of a stretch to say that the fate of well-informed, open, free republics could hinge on the future of libraries. Maureen Sullivan, then-president of the American Library Association and one of the great librarians who give me hope, told me: "The reason I think the future of libraries is so important is because I want to ensure that every child in America has access to the information he or she needs to be well-informed before casting a vote." Our public institutions have every reason to work together on a common, bright, delightful, digital-era future. Libraries matter too much to democracies for us to fail at this task.

Acknowledgments

I owe deep thanks to the many librarians and archivists who have helped me learn about their great institutions and respective professions in the past ten years. All misinterpretations and other errors, however, are mine alone.

My colleagues in the Harvard Library have taught me more about libraries and archives than I ever could have imagined possible. They are too many to include exhaustively by name, but Mike Barker, Cathy Conroy, Kim Dulin, Pam Peifer, and Suzanne Wones (the EC!) deserve special thanks, as do June Casey and Cheryl LaGuardia, with whom I've worked most closely on reference matters. Conversations with members of the Harvard Library Board, including Robert Darnton, Terry Fisher, Alan Garber, Zak Keohane, Stuart Shieber, Jonathan Zittrain, and others, have likewise informed my thinking about libraries.

My colleagues at the Berkman Center for Internet and Society at Harvard University and the Digital Public Library of America team have provided inspiration and help. Dana Walters conducted many fruitful interviews and made essential contributions to the manuscript. Maura Marx (formerly the managing director of the DPLA, now a senior civil servant in the US government) is wonderful, as are Dan Cohen, Sandra Cortesi, Urs Gasser, Emily Gore, Rebekah Heacock, Nathaniel Levy, Momin Malik, Caroline Nolan, David O'Brien, Amy Rudersdorf, Jeffrey Schnapp, David Weinberger (who offered a particularly helpful reading of a draft), and Kenny Whitebloom. Doron Weber deserves special mention: he is first among equals in terms of funders and supporters of the DPLA and a thought partner of the highest order.

My colleagues in the Phillips Academy library—especially Elisabeth Tully (whose comments prompted a near-total rewrite of an early draft of the book), Kathrine Aydelott, Michael Blake, and Jeffrey Marzluft—have been generous with their time and constructive criticism. Lura Sanborn of St. Paul's School read a draft of the book and offered excellent, pointed criticism and ideas for supporting documentation. So, too, have the many public and academic library leaders who have made that process such a fun, creative, and informative one. Maureen Sullivan, former president of the American Library Association and library school dean at Simmons College, has always been a trusted guide in my learning process about libraries, leadership, and much else besides. Michael Kelley of *Library Journal* has kindly enabled me to try out some of the ideas that appear in this book in his publication. Many library and philanthropic leaders helped much more than they know: Julian Aiken, Brian Bannon, Michael Colford, Josh Greenberg, Luis Herrera, Kathryn James, Mary Lee Kennedy, Tony Marx, Sharon O'Connor, Amy Ryan, Andrea Saenz, and Candy Schwartz have had outsized effects on my understanding of these topics.

I am indebted to Michelle Tessler, my agent, who helped to shape the idea into a book. No one is as good (or as tough!) in the service of improving a text as Lara Heimert, publisher of Basic Books, to whom I owe unending gratitude. Katy O'Donnell, Melissa Veronesi, and Cynthia Buck performed masterful work in the line-editing and copyediting stages. I feel blessed to have worked with each of them on this project.

As ever, I owe profound thanks to my family—Catherine, Jack, and Emeline—who seem to have endless patience for book projects, among other diversions from otherwise harmonious domestic life.

Notes

Introduction

1. See, for example, Hina Hirayama, *"With Éclat": The Boston Athenaeum and the Origin of the Museum of Fine Arts, Boston* (University Press of New England, 2003), 11.

2. Abigail A. Van Slyck, *Free to All: Carnegie Libraries and American Culture, 1890–1920* (University of Chicago Press, 1995), 22.

3. Juan Gonzalez and Ginger Adams Otis, "Queens Library Director Thomas Galante Fired for His Wild Spending Habits," *New York Daily News*, December 18, 2014, http://www.nydailynews.com/new-york/queens-library-fires-thomas-galante-wild-spending-article-1.2049422.

Chapter 1: Crisis: A Perfect Storm

1. See Richard A. Danner, "Supporting Scholarship: Thoughts on the Role of the Academic Law Librarian," *Journal of Law and Education* 39, no. 3 (April 2010): 365–386, http://scholarship.law.duke.edu/cgi/viewcontent.cgi?article=2693&context=faculty_scholarship.

2. David Bawden and Lyn Robinson, *Introduction to Information Science* (Neal-Schuman, 2012), 23.

3. R. David Lankes, *The Atlas of New Librarianship* (MIT Press, 2011), 23; Stephen Greenblatt, *The Swerve: How the World Became Modern* (W. W. Norton, 2012).

4. See Kendall F. Svengalis, *Legal Information Buyer's Guide and Reference Manual 2009* (Rhode Island LawPress), 3. Consider also the research published by Bowker, a private firm that periodically issues statistics about the total number of books published; see, for example, "Publishing Market Shows Steady Title Growth in 2011 Fueled Largely by Self-Publishing Sector," Bowker, June 5, 2012, http://www.bowker.com/en-US/aboutus/press_room/2012 /pr_06052012.shtml, and "Self-Publishing Sees Triple-Digit Growth in Just Five Years, Says Bowker," Bowker, October 24, 2012, http:// www.bowker.com/en-US/aboutus/press_room/2012/pr_10242012 .shtml. It is Bowker's combined data that show more than 1 million books being published around the world each year. The Wikipedia page on book publishing was up-to-date at the time of this writing; see "Books Published per Country per Year," Wikipedia, http:// en.wikipedia.org/wiki/Books_published_per_country_per_year. See also Nick Morgan, "Thinking of Self-Publishing Your Book in 2013? Here's What You Need to Know," *Forbes,* January 8, 2013, http://www.forbes.com/sites/nickmorgan/2013/01/08/thinking -of-self-publishing-your-book-in-2013-heres-what-you-need-to -know/.

5. See Kendall F. Svengalis, "Legal Information: Globalization, Conglomerates, and Competition: Monopoly or Free Market," PowerPoint presentation given at the Association of Legal Administrators Annual Conference, July 15, 2007, www.nelawpress.com /AALL2007.ppt.

6. Strictly speaking, the act of placing faculty scholarship in an institutional repository does not constitute "publishing" that information. From the perspective of libraries, however, the place-

ment of articles into public online spaces such as repositories serves at least three key functions: providing access to the work; providing metadata about the work; and preserving the work, at least for some period of time.

7. On the recent and ongoing curricular reforms in Vanderbilt's and Harvard's first-year law programs, see Jonathan D. Glater, "Training Law Students for Real-Life Careers," *New York Times,* October 31, 2007. On curricular reform at US law schools generally, see Toni M. Fine, "Reflections on US Law Curricular Reform," *German Law Journal* 10 (2009): 717–750.

8. Carl A. Yirka, "The Yirka Question and Yirka's Answer: What Should Law Libraries Stop Doing in Order to Address Higher Priority Initiatives?" *AALL (American Association of Law Libraries) Spectrum* (July 2008): 28–32.

9. See Patrick Meyer, "Law Firm Legal Research Requirements for New Attorneys," *Law Library Journal* 101, no. 3 (2009): 297–330; Meyer affirms that "books are far from dead in the law firm setting" (71). John Seely Brown and Paul Duguid, in *The Social Life of Information* (Harvard Business Review Press, 2000, 173–174), describe how, for instance, some scholars reportedly sniff letters in archives for the scent of vinegar to track cholera outbreaks.

10. Consider the WAX initiative carried out by the Harvard University Office for Information Systems; see "Overview: Web Archive Collection Service (WAX)," Harvard University Information Technology, Library Technology Services, http://hul.harvard.edu /ois/systems/wax/.

11. See, among many other sources, Basil Manns and Chadrui J. Shahani, *Longevity of CD Media: Research at the Library of Congress* (Library of Congress, 2003); and Fred R. Byers, *Care and Handling of CDs and DVDs: A Guide for Librarians and Archivists* (Council on Library and Information Resources, 2003).

12. For the argument that several large research libraries ought to commit to retaining certain print collections even post-digitization,

albeit in the context of journals, see Roger C. Schonfeld and Ross Housewright, "What to Withdraw: Print Collections Management in the Wake of Digitization," September 1, 2009, http://www.sr .ithaka.org/research-publications/what-withdraw-print-collections -management-wake-digitization; see also Robert Darnton, *The Case for Books: Past, Present, and Future* (PublicAffairs, 2009).

13. Consider the challenge confronted by the National Archives—especially under National Archivist David Ferriero—in grappling with the email records of US presidents; see, for example, "Memorandum of Understanding on the Clinton-Gore E-mail Records," National Archives, Presidential Libraries and Museums, January 11, 2001, http://www.archives.gov/presidential-libraries/laws/access /email-records-memo.html. For an early discussion of the kinds of interoperability that will be necessary to make a sustainable digital ecosystem for library information succeed, see Andreas Paepcke et al., "Interoperability for Digital Libraries Worldwide," *Communications of the ACM (Association for Computing Machinery)* (April 1998): 33.

14. There is robust debate as to whether law schools in particular are keeping up with these changes; see, for example, the posting of Paul Lippe to AmLaw Daily, "Welcome to the Future: Time for Law School 4.0," June 22, 2009 (http://amlawdaily.typepad.com /amlawdaily/2009/06/school.html), and the many comments it elicited. See also American Association of Law Libraries, *Price Index for Legal Publications,* 6th ed. (2008), available to AALL members at: http://www.aallnet.org/members/price_index-2008.asp.

15. Lisa L. Colangelo, "Budget Cuts Forces Queens Library to Shutter 14 Branches, Cut 300 Words and Reduce Hours," *New York Daily News,* May 18, 2010, http://www.nydailynews.com /new-york/queens/budget-cuts-forces-queens-library-shutter -14-branches-cut-300-workers-reduce-hours-article-1.446195.

16. American Library Association, "Public Library Funding Updates," http://www.ala.org/advocacy/libfunding/public.

17. Michael Kelley, "The New Normal: Annual Library Budgets Survey 2012," *Library Journal,* January 16, 2012, http://lj.library journal.com/2012/01/funding/the-new-normal-annual-library -budgets-survey-2012/.

18. For an example of budget cuts at a university library, see University Libraries, University of Washington, "University Libraries Reduces Journal Subscriptions and Book Orders; Budget Cuts Affect Online as Well as Print Materials," January 4, 2010, http://www.lib.washington.edu/about/news/announcements /journal_subscriptions.

Chapter 2: Customers: How We Use Libraries

1. There is no single, definitive public source of information on ebook sales and usage, but one can cobble together the rough picture by combining a variety of data points. See, for example, Marcia Pledger, "Library Market Leader E-Book Distributor OverDrive Inc. Looks at Schools as the Next Growth Market," *Cleveland Plain Dealer,* July 5, 2013, http://www.cleveland.com/business/index.ssf /2013/07/library_market_leader_e-book_d.html; Ava Seave, "Are Digital Libraries a 'Winner-Takes-All' Market? OverDrive Hopes So," *Forbes,* November 18, 2013, http://www.forbes.com/sites/ava seave/2013/11/18/are-digital-libraries-a-winner-takes-all-market -overdrive-hopes-so/; and "$2 Billion for $1 Billion of Books: The Arithmetic of Library E-Book Lending," Library Renewal, March 5, 2012, http://libraryrenewal.org/2012/03/05/2-billion-for-1-billion -of-books-the-arithmetic-of-library-e-book-lending.

2. Wayne Friedman, "Video-on-Demand Viewing on the Rise," *MediaPost,* April 8, 2014, http://www.mediapost.com/publications /article/223237/video-on-demand-viewing-on-the-rise.html.

3. Libraries, of course, do lend some digital materials, such as ebooks; see Kathryn Zickuhr et al., "Libraries, Patrons, and E-Books," Pew Internet and American Life Project, June 22, 2012,

http://libraries.pewinternet.org/2012/06/22/libraries-patrons-and
-e-books/. There are major stumbling blocks, however, to libraries
becoming the primary mode of distribution for ebooks or on-
demand movies, including both contract law and copyright; this
issue is explored in various places throughout the book.

4. Alison Flood, "Zadie Smith Defends Local Libraries," *The
Guardian,* August 31, 2012, http://www.theguardian.com/books
/2012/aug/31/zadie-smith-defends-local-libraries.

5. See, for example, Kathryn Zickuhr, Lee Rainie, and Kristen
Purcell, "Library Services in the Digital Age," Pew Internet and
American Life Project, January 22, 2013, http://libraries.pewinter
net.org/2013/01/22/library-services/.

6. Ibid.; see also David L. Ulin, "Not Dead Yet: Libraries Still
Vital, Pew Report Finds," *Los Angeles Times,* January 22, 2013,
http://www.latimes.com/features/books/jacketcopy/la-et-jc-pews
-report-on-libraries-is-upbeat-20130119,0,1014616.story.

7. Kathryn Zickuhr et al., "Younger Americans' Reading and
Library Habits," Pew Internet and American Life Project, October
23, 2012, http://libraries.pewinternet.org/2012/10/23/younger
-americans-reading-and-library-habits/; see also Melissa Gross
and Don Latham, "Experiences with and Perceptions of Information: A Phenomenographic Study of First-Year College Students,"
Library Quarterly 81, no. 2 (April 2011): 161–186; Flor Henderson,
Nelson Nunez-Rodriguez, and William Casari, "Enhancing Research Skills and Information Literacy in Community College
Science Students," *The American Biology Teacher* 73, no. 5 (May
2011): 270–275.

8. Alison J. Head and Michael B. Eisenberg, "Balancing Act:
How College Students Manage Technology While in the Library
During Crunch Time," Project Information Literacy Research Report, October 12, 2011, http://projectinfolit.org/images/pdfs/pil
_fall2011_techstudy_fullreport1.2.pdf; Alison J. Head and Michael B. Eisenberg, "Truth Be Told: How College Students Evaluate

and Use Information in the Digital Age," Project Information Literacy Progress Report, November 1, 2010, http://projectinfolit.org/images/pdfs/pil_fall2010_survey_fullreport1.pdf; Alison J. Head and Michael B. Eisenberg, "Lessons Learned: How College Students Seek Information in the Digital Age," Project Information Literacy Progress Report, December 1, 2009, http://projectinfolit.org/images/pdfs/pil_fall2011_techstudy_fullreport1.2.pdf; Henderson et al., "Enhancing Research Skills and Information Literacy in Community College Science Students."

9. Head and Eisenberg, "Truth Be Told"; Head and Eisenberg, "Lessons Learned."

10. Glenn Bull et al., "Connecting Informal and Formal Learning: Experiences in the Age of Participatory Media," *Contemporary Issues in Technology and Teacher Education* 8, no. 2 (2008): 100–107.

11. Mary Madden et al., "Teens and Technology 2013," Pew Internet and American Life Project, March 13, 2013, http://pewinternet.org/Reports/2013/Teens-and-Tech.aspx; Sara Corbett, "Learning by Playing: Video Games in the Classroom," *New York Times Magazine,* September 15, 2010, http://www.nytimes.com/2010/09/19/magazine/19video-t.html?pagewanted=all.

12. Kathryn Zickuhr and Aaron Smith, "Home Broadband 2013," Pew Research Internet Project, August 26, 2013, http://www.pewinternet.org/2013/08/26/home-broadband-2013; US Department of Commerce, National Communications and Information Administration, "Exploring the Digital Nation: Computer and Internet Use at Home," November 2011, http://www.ntia.doc.gov/report/2011/exploring-digital-nation-computer-and-internet-use-home; Ali Modarres, "Beyond the Digital Divide," *National Civic Review* 100, no. 3 (Autumn 2011): 4–7.

13. Susan Crawford, *Captive Audience: The Telecom Industry and Monopoly Power in the New Gilded Age* (Yale University Press, 2012); US Department of Commerce, "Exploring the Digital Nation."

14. Partnership for 21st Century Skills, "Overview of State Leadership Initiative," http://www.p21.org/members-states/partner states.

15. Sara Nephew Hassani, "Locating Digital Divides at Home, Work, and Everywhere Else," *Poetics* 34 (2006): 250–272.

16. American Library Association, "ALA Library Fact Sheet 6: Public Library Use," February 2013, http://www.ala.org/tools/lib factsheets/alalibraryfactsheet06; American Library Association, "ALA Library Fact Sheet 1: Number of Libraries in the United States," February 2013, http://www.ala.org/tools/libfactsheets/ala libraryfactsheet01; and Anton Troianovski, "The Web-Deprived Study at McDonald's," *Wall Street Journal,* January 28, 2013, http://online.wsj.com/article/SB10001424127887324731304578189794161056954.html. The Bill and Melinda Gates Foundation's Global Libraries Initiative, as of this writing, is winding down its operations after a highly successful run of about two decades; see Bill and Melinda Gates Foundation, "What We Do: Global Libraries Strategy Overview," http://www.gatesfoundation.org/What-We-Do/Global-Development/Global-Libraries.

17. Michael McGrath, "Zeroing the Divide: Promoting Broadband Use and Media Savvy in Underserved Communities," *National Civic Review* 100, no. 3 (Autumn 2011): 24–28.

18. Troianovski, "The Web-Deprived Study at McDonald's." See also a study that shows that 80 percent of Americans live within twenty miles of a Starbucks: James A. Davenport, "The United States of Starbucks," *If We Assume,* October 4, 2012, http://www.ifweassume.com/2012/10/the-united-states-of-starbucks.html; McDonald's, "Free Wi-Fi @ McDonald's," http://www.mcdonalds.com/us/en/services/free_wifi.html; and Starbucks Corporation, "2012 Annual Report," http://investor.starbucks.com/phoenix.zhtml?c=99518&p=irol-reportsannual.

19. Fels Research & Consulting, "The Economic Value of the Free Library in Philadelphia," University of Pennsylvania, Fels In-

stitute of Government, October 21, 2010, http://www.freelibrary
.org/about/Fels_Report.pdf.

20. Eszter Hargittai, "Digital Na(t)ives? Variation in Internet Skills
and Uses Among Members of the 'Net Generation,'" *Sociological In-
quiry* 80, no. 1 (February 2010): 92–113; Eszter Hargittai, "Second-
Level Digital Divide: Differences in People's Online Skills," *First
Monday* 7, no. 4 (April 2002), http://firstmonday.org/article/view/942
/864; Jochen Peter and Patti M. Valkenburg, "Adolescents' Internet
Use: Testing the 'Disappearing Digital Divide' Versus the 'Emerging
Digital Differentiation' Approach," *Poetics* 34 (2006): 293–305.

21. Zickuhr et al., "Library Services in the Digital Age."

22. Eszter Hargittai and Gina Walejko, "The Participation Divide:
Content Creation and Sharing in the Digital Age," *Information,
Communication, and Society* 11, no. 2 (2008): 239–256. For a study
that cites studies of variations in the performance of young people
by class and race and sets results in the context of global achievement gaps, see Tony Wagner, *The Global Achievement Gap: Why
Even Our Best Schools Don't Teach the New Survival Skills Our Children Need—and What We Can Do About It* (Basic Books, 2010).

23. Andrew D. Madden, Nigel J. Ford, David Miller, and Philippa
Levy, "Children's Use of the Internet for Information-Seeking:
What Strategies Do They Use, and What Factors Affect Their Per-
formance?" *Journal of Documentation* 62, no. 6 (2006): 744–761;
Andrew D. Madden, Nigel J. Ford, and David Miller, "Information
Resources Used by Children at an English Secondary School: Per-
ceived and Actual Levels of Usefulness," *Journal of Documentation*
63, no. 3 (2007): 340–358.

24. Institute of Museum and Library Services, "Public Libraries
in the United States Survey: Fiscal Year 2010," January 2013,
http://www.imls.gov/assets/1/AssetManager/PLS2010.pdf; Zickuhr et al., "Library Services in the Digital Age"; Kathryn Zickuhr,
Lee Rainie, Kristen Purcell, and Maeve Duggan, "How Americans
Value Public Libraries in Their Communities," Pew Internet and

American Life Project, December 11, 2013, http://libraries.pew
internet.org/2013/12/11/libraries-in-communities/.

25. See, for example, Center for an Urban Future, "Branches of
Opportunity," January 2013, http://nycfuture.org/images_pdfs
/pdfs/BranchesofOpportunity.pdf.

26. Dennis Gaffney, "Why I Love Libraries," ilovelibraries.org,
http://www.ilovelibraries.org/why-i-love-libraries.

Chapter 3: Spaces:
The Connection Between the Virtual and the Physical

1. Notations in the margins of law school casebooks are not
new to this generation of law students. Rather, this tradition goes
back for hundreds of years. In its Historical and Special Collections, the Harvard Law School, among others, has developed a collection of early casebooks from the nineteenth century in which
marginal comments appear regularly.

2. This change to digital textbooks in law will occur in the next
few years. Librarians should play a major role in this design, but if
the past is prologue, it is unlikely that they will. John Mayer of the
nonprofit CALI (Center for Computer-Assisted Legal Instruction)
and Jonathan Zittrain of Harvard Law School have been doing
pioneering work on projects to remake the law school casebook,
and several forward-thinking publishers are experimenting with
new designs, but none is a librarian. In the summer of 2010,
Amazon.com reported that the sales of ebooks for its Kindle device
surpassed sales of hardcovers for the first time. Claire Cain Miller,
"E-Books Top Hardcovers at Amazon," *New York Times*, July 19,
2010, http://www.nytimes.com/2010/07/20/technology/20kindle
.html.

3. Center for an Urban Future, "Branches of Opportunity,"
January 2013, http://nycfuture.org/research/publications/branches
-of-opportunity.

4. For a description of the therapy dog service, see Julian Aiken, "Meet Monty," Yale Law School, Lillian Goldman Law Library, September 19, 2012, http://library.law.yale.edu/news/meet-monty. See also Owen Fletcher, "Check These Out at the Library: Blacksmithing, Bowling, Butchering," *Wall Street Journal,* January 7, 2013, http://online.wsj.com/article/SB10001424127887324677204 578187901423347828.html.

5. See "YouMedia at the Harold Washington Library: Creating Pathways from Interests to Opportunities," Connected Learning, http://connectedlearning.tv/case-studies/youmedia-harold -washington-library-creating-pathways-interests-opportunities; Melissa Gross, Eliza T. Dresang, and Leslie E. Holt, "Children's In-Library Use of Computers in an Urban Public Library," *Library and Information Science Research* 26 (2004): 311–337; Andrew K. Shenton, "Use of School Resource Center-Based Computers in Leisure Time by Teenage Pupils," *Journal of Librarianship and Information Science* 42, no. 2 (2008): 123–137.

6. See the YouMedia Chicago website at http://youmedia chicago.org/ and the Library of Games website at http://library ofgames.org/; see also Dover Town Library, "Gaming," http:// www.dovertownlibrary.org/tech/gaming/.

7. Rikke Magnussen, "Game-Like Technology Innovation Education," *International Journal of Virtual and Personal Learning Environments* 2, no. 2 (April-June 2011): 30–39; Gadi Alexander, Isabelle Eaton, and Kieran Egan, "Cracking the Code of Electronic Games: Some Lessons for Educators," *Teachers College Record* 112, no. 7 (July 2010): 1830–1850.

8. Find Scratch, a venerable and highly successful project of the MIT Media Lab, at http://scratch.mit.edu/. See also Mizuko Ito et al., "Connected Learning: An Agenda for Research and Design," Digital Media and Learning Research Hub, January 2013, http:// dmlhub.net/sites/default/files/ConnectedLearning_report.pdf; Carolyn Sun, "Kansas Boy Gets New Hand, Created at a Library

Makerspace," The Digital Shift, February 11, 2014, http://www
.thedigitalshift.com/2014/02/k-12/library-innovation-leads-new
-hand-kansas-boy/.

9. For discussion of one such conversion in Wisconsin, see
Mark Schaaf, "Signs Point to Old Library's Future," Greenfield
Now, December 7, 2009, http://www.greenfieldnow.com/news
/78731337.html); for a series of related examples, see Larry T. Nix,
"Spend the Night in a Converted Carnegie Library," ilovelibraries
.org, http://www.ilovelibraries.org/articles/featuredstories/carnegie
hotel.

10. Sarah Williams Goldhagen, "The Revolution at Your Community Library: New Media, New Community Centers," The New
Republic, March 9, 2013, http://www.newrepublic.com/article
/112443/revolution-your-community-library#.

11. Jaron Lanier makes this larger point very effectively throughout his book, You Are Not a Gadget: A Manifesto (Vintage, 2011).

12. Center for an Urban Future, "Branches of Opportunity," 3.

Chapter 4: Platforms:
What Cloud Computing Means for Libraries

1. See the American Girl website at http://www.americangirl
.com/ and Innerstar University at http://web.innerstaru.com/.

2. For context and advice from the American Girl company for
parents about the InnerstarU experience for girls, see American
Girl, "Just for Parents," http://web.innerstaru.com/parents.php.

3. Esther Yi, "Inside the Quest to Put the World's Libraries Online," The Atlantic, July 26, 2012, http://www.theatlantic.com
/entertainment/archive/2012/07/inside-the-quest-to-put-the
-worlds-libraries-online/259967/.

4. Robert Darnton has made a similar point: "To keep up with
the flow of publications, libraries must limit the scope of their

acquisitions and cooperate with one another, for no research library can go it alone in the twenty-first century." See "In Defense of the New York Public Library," *The New York Review of Books,* June 7, 2012, http://www.nybooks.com/articles/archives/2012/jun/07/defense-new-york-public-library/.

5. I am not the first person to make this argument, by the way. The author David Weinberger, for instance, has been arguing in favor of libraries as platforms for many years. In fact, a conference entitled "The Library as Platform" took place in Grand Rapids, Michigan, in 2014.

6. Doron Weber, "A Proud Day for the DPLA," DPLA Blog, April 18, 2013, http://dp.la/info/2013/04/18/a-proud-day-for-the-dpla/.

7. See the DPLA website at http://dp.la.

8. For information on hubs, see "Hubs" on the DPLA website at http://dp.la/info/hubs/.

9. See the Minnesota Digital Library's Minnesota Reflections website at http://reflections.mndigital.org/. Listen to the toad at Western Soundscape Archive, "Wyoming Toad 3," http://content.lib.utah.edu/cdm/ref/collection/wss/id/909.

10. I wish I could take credit for the name "Scannebagos," but I can't. The credit belongs to Emily Gore, a digital library pioneer and the founding director of content of the Digital Public Library of America.

11. Jill Cousins, Harry Verwayen, and Mel Collie, "Outline Business Plan for Europeana as a Service of the EDL Foundation," Europeana Think Culture, November 2008, http://pro.europeana.eu/c/document_library/get_file?uuid=0c6c6078-8026-4297-9367-dd6d14b73c2e&groupId=10602.

12. See Europeana Exhibitions, "Leaving Europe: A New Life in America," http://acceptance.exhibit.eanadev.org/exhibits/show/europe-america-en.

Chapter 5: Hacking Libraries: How to Build the Future

1. For many of the studies that make this case in general, consider the collective work of the Benton Foundation; see "Initiatives" at its website, http://benton.org/initiatives. Many studies by the research team at Pew have made similar general conclusions, though their notes provide citations for more specific claims; for examples, see the Pew Research Center website at http://www.pew research.org/.

2. The story of these computing pioneers is told in Steven Levy, *Hackers: Heroes of the Computer Revolution* (O'Reilly Media, 1984).

3. See Hack Library School at http://hacklibschool.wordpress .com/.

4. The idea of rethinking library operations for a digital era is not a new one. Many shrewd observers have made a similar case in recent years. Consider, for instance, Peter Brantley, "Reality Dreams (for Libraries)," Shimenawa, December 29, 2009, http:// peterbrantley.com/reality-dreams-for-libraries-213.

5. For another case for the library as platform, see David Weinberger, "Library as Platform," *Library Journal,* September 4, 2012, http://lj.libraryjournal.com/2012/09/future-of-libraries/by-david -weinberger/.

6. See Cambridge Digital Library, "Trinity College Notebook by Isaac Newton," http://cudl.lib.cam.ac.uk/view/MS-ADD-03996/3.

7. For one of the many articles about map theft, see William Finnegan, "A Theft in the Library: The Case of the Missing Maps," *The New Yorker,* October 17, 2005, 4–78.

8. Many library observers and leaders write about collaboration in libraries. See, for instance, Collaborationista, a blog written by Tracy Thompson-Przylucki, executive director of NELLCO, an international consortium of law libraries, at http://www.collaboration ista.org/.

9. See the OCLC website at http://www.oclc.org/about/default
.htm.

10. See OCLC, "History of the OCLC Research Library Partnership," http://www.oclc.org/research/partnership/history.html.

11. See Steve Kolowich, "Libraries of the Future," *Inside Higher
Ed,* September 24, 2009, http://www.insidehighered.com/news
/2009/09/24/libraries.

12. See Code4Lib, "About," http://code4lib.org/about.

13. See the NEXT Library website at http://www.nextlibrary
.net/.

14. See Christopher Harris, "A Call for 'Blended Funding':
Schools Must Pool Money to Support Common Core," *Library
Journal,* December 10, 2012, http://www.thedigitalshift.com/2012
/12/opinion/the-next-big-thing/enter-blended-funding-schools
-must-pool-money-to-support-common-core-next-big-thing/

15. See IBM, "IBM Big Data and Information Management,"
http://www-01.ibm.com/software/data/bigdata/.

Chapter 6: Networks: The Human Network of Librarians

1. Marilyn Johnson, *This Book Is Overdue! How Librarians and
Cybrarians Can Save Us All* (HarperCollins, 2010).

2. See Sarah Houghton's blog Librarian in Black at http://
librarianinblack.net/librarianinblack/about.

3. For a directory of iSchools, visit the iSchools website at http://
ischools.org/members/directory/.

Chapter 7: Preservation:
Collaboration, Not Competition, to Preserve Culture

1. See a post on a Twitter engineering blog, "New Tweets per
Second Record, and How!" August 16, 2013, https://blog.twitter
.com/2013/new-tweets-per-second-record-and-how.

2. See Brian Lavoie, Lynn Silipigni Connaway, and Lorcan Dempsey, "Anatomy of Aggregate Collections: The Example of Google Print for Libraries," *D-Lib Magazine* 11, no. 9 (September 2005), http://www.dlib.org/dlib/september05/lavoie/09lavoie.html.

3. See HathiTrust Digital Library, "Welcome to the Shared Digital Future," http://www.hathitrust.org/about.

4. See Digital Preservation Network, "The DPN Vision," http://www.dpn.org/about/.

5. Nicholson Baker, *Double Fold: Libraries and the Assault on Paper* (Random House, 2001).

6. See the website of LLMC Digital, http://www.llmc.com/.

7. Nate Hill, Chattanooga Public Library, email to the DPLA content and scope public listserv, March 18, 2013.

8. See Michael Kelley, "Major Maine Libraries, Public and Academic, Collaborate on Print Archiving Project," *Library Journal,* March 15, 2013, http://lj.libraryjournal.com/2013/03/managing-libraries/major-maine-libraries-public-and-academic-collaborate-on-print-archiving-project/; and Center for Research Libraries, Global Resources Network, "Print Archiving Network," http://www.crl.edu/archiving-preservation/print-archives/forum.

9. For an argument that several large research libraries ought to commit to retaining certain print collections even post-digitization, albeit in the context of journals, see Roger C. Schonfeld and Ross Housewright, "What to Withdraw: Print Collections Management in the Wake of Digitization," September 1, 2009, http://www.ithaka.org/ithaka-s-r/research/what-to-withdraw.

Chapter 8: Education: Libraries and Connected Learners

1. See American Library Association, "Number of Libraries in the United States: ALA Library Fact Sheet 1," http://www.ala.org/tools/libfactsheets/alalibraryfactsheet01 (last updated April 2014).

2. See American Library Association, "School Libraries: A Bad Year on the Budget Front, with No End in Sight," 2012, http://www.ala.org/news/mediapresscenter/americaslibraries/soal2012/school-libraries.

3. Several studies have shown a strong correlation between better-staffed and better-funded school libraries and student performance. One researcher in particular, Keith Curry Lance, has conducted studies in multiple states, including Illinois and Indiana, in the past decade. For one such study, see Keith Curry Lance and Linda Hofschire, "Change in School Librarian Staffing Linked with Change in CSAP Reading Performance, 2005 to 2011," Colorado State Library, Library Research Service, January 2012, http://www.lrs.org/documents/closer_look/CO4_2012_Closer_Look_Report.pdf.

4. Urs Gasser et al., "Youth and Digital Media: From Credibility to Information Quality," Berkman Center Research Publication 2012-1, February 16, 2012, http://papers.ssrn.com/sol3/papers.cfm?abstract_id=2005272.

5. See Mt. Diablo Unified School District, "Key Points in English Language Arts," http://www.mdusd.org/departments/saas/commoncore/key_points. For full details on the Common Core Standards in English Language Arts, see: http://www.corestandards.org/ELA-Literacy/.

6. As of 2014, the Common Core standards had been formally adopted, in part or in full, by forty-five states and three territories. See http://www.corestandards.org/in-the-states.

7. For general information, see Common Core State Standards Initiative, "Standards in Your State," http://www.corestandards.org/.

8. On the topic of implementing the Common Core, see Rebecca Hill, "All Aboard! Implementing Common Core Offers School Librarians an Opportunity to Take the Lead," *School Library Journal*, March 30, 2012, http://www.slj.com/2012/03/standards/common-core/all-aboard-implementing-common-core-offers

-school-librarians-an-opportunity-to-take-the-lead/; and Myra Zarnowski, Marc Aronson, and Mary Ann Cappiello, "On Common Core: Talking About Nonfiction," *School Library Journal,* February 4, 2013, http://www.slj.com/2013/02/curriculum-connections /on-common-core-talking-about-nonfiction/.

9. See Common Core State Standards Initiative, "Grade 3 [Mathematics]: Introduction," http://www.corestandards.org /Math/Content/3/introduction/.

10. Thomas Jefferson, letter to Isaac McPherson, August 13, 1813, available at http://press-pubs.uchicago.edu/founders/documents /a1_8_8s12.html.

11. See Advances in AP, "AP US History, 2014–2015," http:// advancesinap.collegeboard.org/history/us-history. "This rebalanced focus is reflected in the content weighting of the new AP US History program, reducing the time spent on the 19th century to increase the focus on early and recent American history."

12. For statistics on the size and scale of the nation's community colleges, see American Association of Community Colleges, "Community College Trends and Statistics," http://www.aacc.nche.edu /AboutCC/Trends/Pages/default.aspx.

13. Jennifer Arnold, "The Other Academic Library: Librarianship at the Community College," Career Strategies for Librarians, May 2005, http://www.liscareer.com/arnold_commcoll.htm.

14. See, for example, the annual results of the Organization for Economic Cooperation and Development (OECD) Program for International Student Assessment (PISA) study at http://www.oecd .org/pisa/.

15. See for more information on the Amplify tablet, see http:// www.amplify.com/tablet/.

16. Jenny Xie, "Technology in Schools Still Subject to Digital, Income Divides," PBS, March 1, 2013, http://www.pbs.org/mediashift /2013/03/technology-in-schools-still-subject-to-digital-income -divides060.html.

17. Quoted at John S. and James L. Knight Foundation, which he and his brother created (and of which I am a trustee), http://www .knightfoundation.org/about/informed-and-engaged-communities/.

Chapter 9: Law: Why Copyright and Privacy Matter So Much

1. This quotation by John MacArthur Maguire is enshrined on a plaque that hangs in the Harvard Law School Library. See Harvard Law School Library, "Ask a Librarian," http://asklib.law .harvard.edu/a.php?qid=37313.

2. *Library Journal*'s periodic ebook survey makes this point: see "Ebook Usage in US Public Libraries," The Digital Shift, 2012, http://www.thedigitalshift.com/research/ebook-usage-reports /public/.

3. The fair use doctrine functions as an exception, or a limitation, to the rights of copyright holders. Fair use allows people other than the copyright holder to make various uses of copyrighted material without express permission of the copyright holder. Classic examples include parodies, social commentary, and many educational uses. The fair use doctrine, which takes the form of a four-factor balancing test, can be found in Section 107 of the US Copyright Act. For a reliable source for the text of the law as well as helpful contextual information, see Cornell University Law School's excellent Legal Information Institute website at http://www.law .cornell.edu/uscode/text/17/107. See also the ALA's web page devoted to the first sale doctrine at http://www.ala.org/advocacy /copyright/firstsale.

4. See Section 1201 of the US Copyright Act on the circumvention of copyright protection systems on Cornell's Legal Information Institute site at http://www.law.cornell.edu/uscode/text/17 /1201.

5. For a copy of the US District Court's order see http://digital commons.law.scu.edu/cgi/viewcontent.cgi?article=1334&context

=historical. For helpful context, see a blog post by Venkat Balasu-bramani, with comments from Eric Goldman, "First Sale Doctrine Doesn't Allow Resale of Digital Songs—Capitol Records v. ReDigi," Technology and Marketing Law Blog, April 5, 2013, http://blog .ericgoldman.org/archives/2013/04/first_sale_doct.htm. For two contemporary analyses of the issues at stake, see David Ben Salem, "Capitol Records LLC v. ReDigi Inc.: The Applicability of the First Sale Doctrine to Digital Music," Innovation Law Blog, October 24, 2012, http://innovationlawblog.org/2012/10/capitol-records-llc-v -redigi-inc-the-applicability-of-the-first-sale-doctrine-to-digital -music/; and Terry Hart, "Previewing Capitol Records v. ReDigi," Copyhype, September 24, 2012, http://www.copyhype.com/2012/09 /previewing-capitol-records-v-redigi/.

6. See David O'Brien, Urs Gasser, and John Palfrey, "E-Books in Libraries: A Briefing Document Developed in Preparation for a Workshop on E-Lending in Libraries," Berkman Center Research Publication 2012-15, July 1, 2012, http://ssrn.com/abstract=211 1396.

7. William W. "Terry" Fisher has developed an extensive model for an alternative compensation system for movies and music in the digital era; see chapter 6 of his book *Promises to Keep: Technology, Law, and the Future of Entertainment* (Stanford University Press, 2004). Fisher's model could be adapted to the book context as a way to test the theory.

8. DPLA participants, led by Berkeley's Pam Samuelson and Columbia's Jim Neal, have been exploring innovative legal approaches to the problems facing libraries in a digital age through the DPLA's "Legal Issues" workstream; see http://dp.la/wiki /Legal_Issues. The Berkeley Digital Library Copyright Project has produced a series of pathbreaking white papers that explore solutions to these issues and submitted them to the Copyright Office for consideration; see David Hansen et al., Berkeley Digital Library Copyright Project, memo to Karyn Temple Claggett, US Copy-

right Office, February 4, 2013, http://www.copyright.gov/orphan /comments/noi_10222012/Berkeley-Digital-Library-Copyright -Project.pdf. See also Michael Kelley, "All 50 State Librarians Vote to Form Alliance with Internet Archive's Open Library," The Digital Shift, November 4, 2011, http://www.thedigitalshift.com/2011 /11/ebooks/all-50-state-librarians-vote-to-form-alliance with -internet-archives-open-library/; and Open Library's website at http://www.openlibrary.org.

9. Scott Sayare, "France to Digitize Its Own Literary Works," *New York Times,* December 14, 2009, http://www.nytimes.com /2009/12/15/world/europe/15france.html?_r=0.

10. See "Scandinavian Digital Libraries and Projects," WessWeb, http://wessweb.info/index.php/Scandinavian_Digital_Libraries _and_Projects.

11. Most of the essential reports on this topic are in Dutch; see, for example, Robertine Romeny, "Wet staat uitlenen e-boeken niet toe," Boek Blad, February 27, 2013, http://www.boekblad.nl/wet -staat-uitlenen-e-boeken-niet-toe.203303.lynkx. One of the few reports published in English is Gary Price, "Netherlands: Government Report Says Dutch Libraries Cannot Lend Ebooks," *Library Journal* InfoDocket, February 27, 2013, http://www.infodocket .com/2013/02/27/netherlands-government-report-says-dutch -libraries-cannot-lend-ebooks/.

12. Aaron Tan, "NLB to Add 820,000 E-Books to Collection," AsiaOne Science & Tech, March 11, 2013, http://news.asiaone .com/News/Latest%2BNews/Science%2Band%2BTech/Story/A1 Story20130310-407554.html.

13. See John P. Wilkin, "Bibliographic Indeterminacy and the Scale of Problems and Opportunities of 'Rights' in Digital Collection Building," Council on Library and Information Resources "Ruminations" series, February 2011, http://www.clir.org/pubs/ruminations /01wilkin/wilkin.html; see also Naomi Korn and Emma Beer, "Briefing Paper on Managing Orphan Works," JISC (Joint Information

Systems Committee), March 2011, http://www.jisc.ac.uk/media
/documents/publications/programme/2011/scaorphanworksbp.pdf.

14. See Justice Louis Brandeis's opinion in *Olmstead v. the United States* (1928) at http://caselaw.lp.findlaw.com/cgi-bin/get case.pl?court=US&vol=277&invol=438.

15. See American Library Association, "Privacy and Confidentiality," http://www.ala.org/advocacy/privacyconfidentiality/privacy /privacyconfidentiality.

Chapter 10: Conclusion: What's at Stake

1. Kathryn Zickuhr et al., "How Americans Value Public Libraries in Their Communities," Pew Internet and American Life Project, December 11, 2013, http://libraries.pewinternet.org/2013 /12/11/libraries-in-communities/.

2. Marilyn Johnson, *This Book Is Overdue! How Librarians and Cybrarians Can Save Us All* (HarperCollins, 2010), 12.

3. Jeanniey Mullen, "How Libraries Thrive as Technology Advances," Huffington Post, February 13, 2013, http://www.huffington post.com/jeanniey-mullen/library-technology_b_2671383.html.

4. At a conference of librarians, such a suggestion would immediately give rise to claims that Carnegie was a controversial figure, at best. My point here is not so much that we need a particular industrialist to choose a new design for a particular kind of library, but rather that there is an extraordinary opportunity for a philanthropist or two to do for libraries in the digital age what Carnegie did a century ago for libraries in the analog age. Carnegie Corporation remains an important supporter of libraries, though its mission has broadened (to include, for instance, support for higher education in Eurasia). The Sloan Foundation, the Arcadia Fund, the Mellon Foundation, the Knight Foundation (whose board I chair), the Revson Foundation, the Gates Foundation (until its recent announcement that it would abandon library funding), and

others have already made enormous and important contributions to the future of libraries that cannot be discounted. A major, concerted investment is needed for libraries to thrive in a digital era. The opportunity for a large donor to commit—at the same scale as Carnegie's original gifts—to making a transformative set of investments in libraries, archives, and historical societies is exciting to contemplate and necessary if libraries are to make the successful transition to a digital-plus era soon.

5. StackView has been configured in multiple places; see, for example, Cornell University Library, "Virtual Shelf Browser Beta," http://stackview.library.cornell.edu/.

6. William Gibson, "The Science in Science Fiction (interview)," *Talk of the Nation,* National Public Radio, November 30, 1999, http://www.npr.org/templates/story/story.php?storyId=1067220.

7. Abigail Van Slyck, *Free to All: Carnegie Libraries and American Culture, 1890–1920* (University of Chicago Press, 1995), 26.

8. From the broadcaster's remarks in connection with the American Library Association's 1995 "Libraries Change Lives" Campaign.

Selected Bibliography

The digital-era challenge of cataloging materials and creating bibliographies affects me here, just as it does the professional librarians I so admire. There is simply too much wonderful material on the topic of the future of libraries for me to record it all, at one moment in time, for reference. Instead, I point to some sources that have been especially useful to me during the process of researching, thinking about, and writing this book. (All web pages listed in this bibliography and in the notes were accessed on January 3, 2014.)

Largest Influences

It should come as no surprise that there are many illuminating books written about libraries and librarians, as well as about information and knowledge, in the past, present, and future. Here are citations to a few that have been the greatest influences on my own thinking during the research and writing of this book.

The title most immediately comparable to this book is Nicholson Baker's *Double Fold: Libraries and the Assault on Paper* (Vintage, 2002). Baker's book is particularly apt as a comparison because, as I do in this book, he celebrates the importance of libraries and also takes a "tough love" approach. The strong response to this important book has been both positive and negative, almost all of it constructive; the debate Baker provoked, especially on the topic of preservation of materials in print and digital formats, has been an important one. I hope that this book might likewise point to the need to emphasize preservation in a digital era and the gap between our current spending and the scale of the problem.

Another recent and highly relevant book is Marilyn Johnson's *This Book Is Overdue! How Librarians and Cybrarians Can Save Us All* (HarperCollins, 2010), which evokes joy in the reader as she tells stories about librarians in this time of transition. I enjoyed and admire this book very much; I just fear that it is an incomplete narrative, lacking a sense of threat from the external forces bearing down on today's libraries. If Johnson is right and I am not, I will be very pleased to be proved to have been on the wrong side of this particular debate.

From the recent academic literature, I would suggest three books in particular. Robert Darnton's *A Case for Books: Past, Present, and Future* (PublicAffairs, 2009), a compilation of essays written over several years about books and libraries, celebrates books and libraries while asking the right hard questions about the present and future. Much of Professor Darnton's work as a historian concerns the history of books, publishing, libraries, and their connection to democratic systems. I have been deeply influenced by his research and writings. R. David Lankes's *The Atlas of New Librarianship* (MIT Press, 2011) is worthy of hours of reading, general enjoyment, and reflection. Professor Lankes's *Atlas* is a huge treatise—ambitious in form, substance, and sheer reach— that richly rewards the time invested in its pages. Just as beautiful, only in a different way, is *The Library: A World History* by James W. P. Campbell, with photographs by Will Pryce (University of Chicago Press, 2013).

The philosophy behind libraries and information sciences is highly relevant to my book, though its influence may not be evident at first read. The works of David Weinberger, including *Everything Is Miscellaneous* (Times Books, 2007) and *Too Big to Know* (Basic Books, 2012), are essential to this literature. Weinberger is especially thoughtful in how he explores and imagines the broad information ecosystem. In addition to these books, Weinberger has written many essays and blog posts that have influenced my thinking greatly, such as "Library as Platform," published September 4, 2012, by *Library Journal* at http://lj.libraryjournal.com/2012/09/future-of-libraries/by-david-weinberger/. I think Weinberger is quite right, here and elsewhere, and I view his work as the most relevant and useful of the philosophical takes on information and knowledge in a digital age. I should add that I've worked closely with David and admire him greatly, so I'm biased when I talk about his writing.

While I do not spend any time in this text explicitly grappling with the long and rich philosophy of information science, I draw much from works as varied as those by Georg Wilhelm Friedrich Hegel, Michel Foucault, Jacques Derrida, Jürgen Habermas, and Hannah Arendt. In myriad and sometimes conflicting ways, this rich literature on topics of political democracy, discourse, and knowledge lies behind the core arguments in this book. The connections don't always rise in obvious ways to the surface, but I acknowledge the importance and profound influence of these philosophers on my worldview when it comes to libraries, knowledge, and information.

There are many histories of libraries and books that have informed my understanding of libraries in the present and future. Matthew Battles's *Library: An Unquiet History* (W. W. Norton, 2003) tells the history of libraries in a compelling fashion. Though not directly on the same topic, Simon Winchester's *The Meaning of Everything* (Oxford University Press, 2003) tells a story that appeals to an audience similar to the one I write for here. Ian McNeely and Lisa Wolverton's *Reinventing Knowledge: From Alexandria to the Internet* (W. W. Norton, 2008) is a scholarly and historical look at similar themes, focused on the past rather than the future of knowledge.

Other books especially relevant to my topic, from various angles, include: James Gleick, *The Information: A History, a Theory, a Flood* (Vintage, 2011); Jaron Lanier, *You Are Not a Gadget* (Vintage, 2011); Mary Antin, *The Promised Land* (Penguin Classics, 1997); Ann Blair, *Too Much to Know* (Yale University Press, 2010); Dora Thornton, *The Scholar in His Study* (Yale University Press, 1997); and Bruno Latour, *Laboratory Life: The Construction of Scientific Facts* (Princeton University Press, 1986).

The Web and Periodicals: Too Many, Too Big, Too Much to Know

The web, too, is home to a great deal of writing on similar themes. There are far too many to cite here. Consider, however, Lucas Kavner, "Library Budget Cuts Threaten Community Services Across Country," Huffington Post, November 16, 2011, http://www.huffingtonpost.com/2011/11/16/can-the-american-library-_n_1096484.html; the series of essays entitled "Do We Still Need Libraries?" on the "Room for Debate" page of the *New York Times,* December 27, 2012, http://www.nytimes.com/roomfordebate/2012/12/27/do-we-still-need-libraries; and a roundup of "future of the library" type blog posts and white papers by Justine Hyde, "Libraries of the Future?" Hub & Spoke: Justine Hyde, January 9, 2013, http://justinehyde.wordpress.com/2013/01/09/101/.

Periodicals and blogs help enormously in trying to keep up with the latest thinking on libraries and librarians as it evolves. During the last several years of working on this project, I have religiously read *Library Journal, School Library Journal, American Libraries,* and the *Chronicle of Higher Education*'s library reporting, as well as the blogs and video productions of Peter Brantley, Sherry Gick (The Library Fanatic), Sarah Houghton (Librarian in Black), Eli Neiburger, David Rothman, Jessamyn West ("putting the rarin back in librarian since 1999"), Tiffany Whitehead (Mighty Little Librarian), Matthew Winner (The Busy Librarian), and many others. For an excellent list of sources, see the winners of the EduBlog Awards for library blogging at "The Best Library/Librarian Blogs, 2012," The EduBlog Awards, http://edublogawards.com /2012awards/best-library-librarian-blog/.

Helpful Books, Research Reports, and Other Materials

By way of citation about citations, I did some of my research for this book in the context of preparing to teach a class, "Bibliotheca," with Professor Jeffrey Schnapp at Harvard's Graduate School of Design in the fall of 2011. The influence of a design sensibility, from which I have learned much, is plain from this reading list; otherwise, the list is eclectic, reflecting not so much anyone's idea of a canon as the interdisciplinary nature of this topic. I worked initially from a version of Professor Schnapp's course reading list, from which I then made some additions and subtractions, with help from friendly librarians such as June Casey of the Harvard Law School Library. I also admit to being partial to the works published by the MIT Press, which are well represented here.

American Library Association. "Library Bill of Rights." *ALA Bulletin* 42 (July-August 1948): 285.
American Library Association. "Library Statistics." Available at: http://www.ala.org/research/librarystats.

Arendt, Hannah. *The Human Condition.* University of Chicago Press, 1958.

Baird, Georges. *The Space of Appearance.* MIT Press, 1995.

Banfield, Edward. *The Public Library and the City.* MIT Press, 1965.

Barzun, Jacques. *From Dawn to Decadence.* HarperCollins, 2000.

Bloch, Howard, and Carla Hesse. *Future Libraries.* University of California Press, 1995.

Campbell, James W. P. *The Library: A World History.* University of Chicago Press, 2013.

Casson, Lionel. *Libraries of the Ancient World.* Yale University Press, 2002.

Cohen, Daniel, and Roy Rosenzweig. *Digital History: A Guide to Gathering, Preserving, and Presenting the Past on the Web.* University of Pennsylvania Press, 2005.

Conaway, James. *America's Library: The Story of the Library of Congress, 1800–2000.* Yale University Press, 2000.

Darnton, Robert. *The Case for Books: Past, Present, and Future.* PublicAffairs, 2009.

———. "Digitize, Democratize: Libraries and the Future of Books." 25th Annual Horace S. Manges Lecture, Columbia University School of Law, April 2, 2012.

Dewey, John. *Democracy and Education: An Introduction to the Philosophy of Education.* Macmillan, 1916.

Dickson, Paul. *The Library in America: A Celebration in Words and Pictures.* Facts on File Publications, 1986.

Earnshaw, Rae, and John Vince, eds. *Digital Convergence: Libraries of the Future.* Springer, 2008.

Eco, Umberto, and Jean-Claude Carrière. *This Is Not the End of the Book.* Harvill Secker, 2011.

Edwards, Brian, with Biddy Fisher. *Libraries and Learning Resource Centres.* Architectural Press, 2002.

Epstein, Jason. "Books @ Google." *New York Review of Books* (October 19, 2006): 23–25.

Glazer, Nathan, and Mark Lilla. *The Public Face of Architecture: Civic Spaces and Public Spaces.* Free Press, 1987.

Goode, Luke. *Jürgen Habermas: Democracy and the Public Sphere.* Pluto Press, 2005.

Greenblatt, Stephen. *The Swerve: How the World Became Modern.* W. W. Norton, 2012.

Habermas, Jürgen. *Democracy and the Public Sphere.* Pluto Press, 1971.

———. "The Ambivalent View of the Public Sphere in the Theory of Liberalism." In *The Structural Transformation of the Public Sphere,* translated by Tomas Burger with the assistance of Frederick Lawrence. MIT Press, 1989.

Hesse, Carla. "Books in Time." In *The Future of the Book,* edited by Geoffrey Nunberg. University of California Press, 1997.

Heuer, Kenneth. *City of the Stargazers.* Charles Scribner's Sons, 1972.

Hirayama, Hina. *"With Éclat": The Boston Athenaeum and the Origin of the Museum of Fine Arts, Boston.* University Press of New England, 2003.

Höfer, Candida. *Libraries.* Schirmer/Mosel Verlag Gmbh, 2006.

Johnson, Steven. *Future Perfect: The Case for Progress in a Networked Age.* Riverhead, 2012.

Jones, Theodore. *Carnegie Libraries Across America: A Public Legacy.* John Wiley & Sons, 1997.

Keith, William. *Democracy as Discussion: Civic Education and the American Forum Movement.* Lexington Books, 2007.

Khan, Salman. *The One World Schoolhouse: Education Reimagined.* Twelve, 2012.

Koolhaas, Rem, with OMA/AMO. *Content.* Taschen, 2003.

Kranich, Nancy. *Libraries and Democracy: The Cornerstones of Liberty.* American Library Association, 2001.

Learned, William. *The American Public Library and the Diffusion of Knowledge.* Harcourt, Brace and Co., 1924.

LeFevre, Camille. "Texas Transformation: A Former Big-Box Grocery Store Gets New Life as a Thriving Public Library." *Architecture Minnesota* 30, no. 6 (November 2004): 44–47.

Lerner, Fred. *The Story of Libraries: From the Invention of Writing to the Computer Age,* 2nd ed. Continuum, 2009.

MacLeish, Archibald. "The Librarian and the Democratic Process." *ALA Bulletin* 34 (June 1940): 385–388, 421–222.

McLuhan, Marshall. *Understanding Me: Lectures and Interviews,* edited by Stephanie McLuhan and David Staines. MIT Press, 2003.

Milner, Henry. *Civic Literacy: How Informed Citizens Make Democracy Work.* University Press of New England, 2002.

Mitchell, Carolyn, et al. "Reading Habits in Different Communities." Pew Research Internet Project, December 20, 2012. Available at: http://libraries.pewinternet.org/2012/12/20/reading-habits-in-different-communities/.

Mitchell, William. *City of Bits: Space, Place, and the Infobahn.* MIT Press, 1996.

———. *E-Topia.* MIT Press, 2000.

———. *ME ++: The Cyborg Self and the Networked City.* MIT Press, 2003.

———. *Placing Words: Symbols, Space, and the City.* MIT Press, 2005.

Molz, Redmond Kathleen, and Phyllis Dain. *Civic Space/Cyberspace: The American Public Library in the Digital Age.* MIT Press, 1999.

Moore, Charles. *You Have to Pay for Public Life: Selected Essays,* edited by Kevin Keim. MIT Press, 2001.

Murray, Stuart A. P. *The Library: An Illustrated History.* Skyhorse Publishing, 2009.

Newhouse, Victoria. *Towards a New Museum,* expanded edition. Monacelli Press, 2006.

Pawley, Christine. *Reading Places: Literacy, Democracy, and the Public Library in Cold War America.* University of Massachusetts Press, 2010.

Petroski, Henry. *The Book on the Bookshelf.* Knopf, 1999.

Pew Research Internet Project. "Internet & Tech: Libraries" (studies on library usage, organized by topic; see, for example, the entry here for Carolyn Mitchell et al.). Available at: http://pewinternet.org/Topics/Activities-and-Pursuits/Libraries.aspx?typeFilter=5.

Preer, Jean. "Exploring the American Idea at the New York Public Library." *American Studies* 42, no. 3 (Fall 2001): 135–154.

———. "Promoting Citizenship: How Librarians Helped Get Out the Vote in the 1952 Election." *Libraries and the Cultural Record* 43, no. 1 (2008): 1–28.

Putnam, Robert. *Bowling Alone.* Simon & Schuster, 2000.

Ripley, Cynthia. "The Power of Libraries." *Urban Land* 62, no. 10 (October 2003): 96–98.

Samuel, Julian. *The Library in Crisis: A Film Documentary.* Montreal, 2002. Available at: http://www.julianjsamuel.com/films/the-library-in-crisis-2002/.

Sapp, Greg. *A Brief History of the Future of Libraries: An Annotated Bibliography.* Scarecrow Press, 2002.

Schnapp, Jeffrey and Matthew Battler. *The Library Beyond the Book.* Harvard University Press, 2014.

Schwartz, Candy. "Digital Libraries: An Overview." *Journal of Academic Librarianship* 26, no. 6 (November 2000): 385–393.

Staikos, Konstantinos Sp. *The Great Libraries: From Antiquity to the Renaissance (3000 BC to AD 1600).* Oak Knoll Press and British Library, 2000.

Stein, Karen D. "Next Century's Library—Today." *Architectural Record* 184, no. 9 (September 1996): 84–91.

Suber, Peter. *Open Access.* MIT Press, 2012.

Thorburn, David, and Henry Jenkins. *Democracy and New Media.* MIT Press, 2003.

Vaidhyanathan, Siva. *The Googlization of Everything (and Why We Should Worry).* University of California Press, 2011.

Van Slyck, Abigail. *Free to All: Carnegie Libraries and American Culture, 1890–1920.* University of Chicago Press, 1995.

West, Jessamyn C. *Without a Net: Librarians Bridging the Digital Divide.* Libraries Unlimited, 2011.

Willinsky, John. *The Access Principle: The Case for Open Access to Research and Scholarship.* MIT Press, 2009.

Wolf, Maryanne. *Proust and the Squid: The Story and Science of the Reading Brain.* HarperPerennial, 2008.

Wright, Alex. *Glut: Mastering Information Through the Ages.* Joseph Henry Press, 2007.

Index

271

Index

Index

Index

Index